THE
HISTORY
OF THE
WORLD
QUIZ BOOK

1,000 QUESTIONS AND ANSWERS
TO TEST YOUR KNOWLEDGE

Meredith MacArdle

MICHAEL O'MARA BOOKS

First published in Great Britain in 2018 by
Michael O'Mara Books Limited
9 Lion Yard
Tremadoc Road
London SW4 7NQ

Papers used by Michael O'Mara Books Limited are natural, recyclable products made from wood grown in sustainable forests. The manufacturing processes conform to the environmental regulations of the country of origin.

ISBN 978-1-78243-900-4 paperback print format
ISBN 978-1-78243-933-2 in ebook format

2 3 4 5 6 7 8 9 10

Designed and typeset by DESIGN 23
Cover design by Patrick Knowles
Cover image: *Europa recens descripta*, ca. 1644 by Willem Janz. Blaeu / Public Domain
Maps drawn by David Woodroffe

Printed and bound by CPI Group (UK) Ltd, Croydon CR0 4YY

www.mombooks.com

CONTENTS

INTRODUCTION

In his 1953 novel, *The Go-Between*, British author L. P. Hartley wrote, 'The past is a foreign country: they do things differently there.'

The past is a country that many of us enjoy visiting, again and again. Whether watching a costume drama on television, or reading the latest research by historians and archaeologists, history fascinates and absorbs us and belongs to us all. The world's many, vivid cultures are built from centuries of human endeavour and form the foundations of our modern lives. Although history reveals many battles and conflicts, there were peaceable events, too, as well as periods of transformation in the arts and sciences, and in the way our societies evolved.

This book explores all eras and nations, with a focus on major events and those prominent people who left their mark on international history. If you feel you know a lot about a particular period or country, you might be able to answer some questions easily. But there will be plenty more challenging questions to test your knowledge of who did what, when, and why?

Welcome to 5,500 years of questions.

CHAPTER 1

3500 BC–799 BC

1. In 3500 BC, people were still mainly using stone tools (along with bone, antler and wood), so what period of human development is that considered to be? *New Stone Age* *Neolithic*

2. By 3500 BC, people living in small communities in the Alps were building distinctive houses on the edges of lakes and rivers. What were these buildings?
A Round towers **B** Huts on stilts C House barges

3. Although stone was the main tough material used, a metal was also being used in some parts of the world before 3500 BC. What metal was this? *Copper* ~~Bronze~~

4. In which geological regions did the first civilizations develop?
A Mountain tops B Prairies and plains
C River valleys

5. The earliest known civilization in the Americas is the Norte Chico culture that flourished in Peru between about 3500 BC to 1800 BC. They created several monumental structures including pyramids, earthwork platform mounds and, in contrast, what else?
A Obelisks **B** Large, sunken, circular plazas
C Round towers

6. By 3500 BC, the Chinese were tending a small creature and making cloth from it. What was it and what was the material it provided?

7. What was the first food crop that was domesticated in the Americas?
A Wheat **B** Maize **C** Rice

8. Where was Mesopotamia, home to the ancient civilizations of Sumer, Babylon and Assyria?
A Turkey **B** Iran **C** Iraq

9. Around 3500 BC, people in Peru were using which animals for transportation?

10. Ancient stone circles are found in many countries. Is Stonehenge in England (below) a unique stone circle?

11. True or false? Chopsticks were used in ancient China probably well before 3500 BC? ✓

12. Sometime probably between 3239 and 3105 BC, who tried to cross the Alps along the border of modern Austria and Italy, but died on the mountains?

13. This individual had body ornaments that are common around the world today. What were they?

14. Around 3200 BC, the Mesopotamians invented a new way to travel or transport materials. What was it?

15. What is the name of this style of writing, developed by the Sumerians around 3200 BC, which was commonly created by pressing a wedge-shaped tool into wet clay tablets.

16. By 3200 BC, farmers along the Nile in Egypt recognized that the annual flooding of the Nile river is marked by the first seasonal appearance at dawn of which star?
A Sirius B Polaris C Alpha Centauri.

17. The ancient Egyptian dynasties are divided into three main groups. Were they

  A Kingdoms **B** Empires **C** Houses?

18. What name is given to the periods of unrest and division in between the major Egyptian dynastic eras?

Intermediate

19. The passage grave at Newgrange in Ireland, dating to about 3200 BC, was built so that the sun would shine along its passage and into the burial chamber on which day of the year?

winter solstice

20. What is the name of the Neolithic village on Orkney, Scotland, dating to about 3100 BC, where most of the house furnishings – beds, shelves, tables, etc. – were made of stone, since there was a lack of trees on the island?

Skara Brae

21. Where is this stone circle known as Rujm el-Hiri (Stone Heap of the Wild Cat) or Gilgal Refaim (Wheel of Ghosts), built around 3000–2700 BC?

  A Hong Kong **B** Sweden **C** The Golan Heights, Syria/Israel

22. Built around 3000 BC, the Great Dolmen of Zambujeiro in Portugal is the largest single-chambered burial mound in Europe, lined with stones up to eight metres (26 feet) high. True or false? Because of the size of the stones, the archaeologist who explored it in the 1960s used dynamite to access the chamber. *T*

23. Before 3000 BC, which two precious metals were being crafted by humans? *Gold + Silver*

24. About 3000 BC, people in Somalia domesticated which animals? Other people in Africa quickly adopted the same practice.
A Wolves **B** Camels **C** Cats

25. What was the first form of political and social organization in the Sumerian civilization?
A Widespread empires **B** City-states **C** Travelling royal courts

26. Where is the world's largest prehistoric stone circle? *Avebury*

27. What is the meaning of the ancient Egyptian word 'pharaoh'? *Great house*

28. Around 3050 BC, which Egyptian pharaoh united Upper and Lower Egypt into one land and founded the first dynasty of the united Egypt? *Narmer*

29. What important Mesopotamian city lasted for more than two thousand years, was developed by kings such as Sennacherib and Ashurbanipal and contained a great ancient library?
A Alexandria **B** Byblos **C** Nineveh

30. What was the earliest European civilization, flourishing from around 2700 BC to 1500 BC in the Mediterranean area and typified on Crete? *Minoan*

31. In wall paintings and in sculpture, this civilization recorded an unusual form of either entertaining acrobats or ritual performance involving a large and dangerous animal. What was it?

32. True or false? A script from this civilization, known as Linear A, has not yet been deciphered.

33. What was the largest known centre of this civilization?

34. Which weapons were widely associated with the Bronze Age in Europe?

35. Which bronze items typify the Bronze Age in China?
A Vessels **B** Shields **C** Helmets

36. Which Chinese dynasty is particularly associated with the Bronze Age? *Shang*

37. Where are these prehistoric standing stones, part of the largest collection in the world? *Carnac, Brittany France*

38. True or false? The first records of war were carved on Sumerian stones around 2700 BC. *T*

39. Living from 2667 BC to 2648 BC, the earliest known named architect built the first pyramid in Egypt for his pharaoh, Djoser, and became venerated as a god in Memphis for his other skills as a physician. Who was he?
A Ramesses **B** Ptolemy **C** Imhotep

40. What was the capital city of Egypt during the Old Kingdom period from 2663 to 2195 BC?
A Alexandria **B** Cairo **C** Memphis

41. In what modern countries were the majority of the cities of the Indus Valley civilization that was at its height between 2600 and 1800 BC? *INDIA + PAKISTAN*

42. Which covered the largest area of land, ancient Egypt or the Indus Valley civilization?

43. Around 2500 BC, the semi-legendary Chinese emperor Huangdi and his wife Lei Zu are supposed to have invented several of the trappings of civilization: a primitive form of writing, a calendar and ceramics. Huangdi was known by another title, based on the colour of the earth around one of China's major rivers, what was it?
A The Purple Emperor **B** The Yellow Emperor
C The Red Emperor

44. What sanitation feature was found in many houses in the Indus Valley civilization? *Flush toilets*

45. True or false? Archaeologists think that the primary purpose of huge, defensive walls around many cities of the Indus Valley civilization was to resist floods. *T*

46. The cities of the Indus Valley civilization were occupied for only about 700 years. Why do archaeologists think that city life may have ended there?

A They were invaded by conquerors from the south
B The rivers dried up and could not sustain concentrated populations
C Civil wars between the cities

47. True or false? This Indus or Harappan script from the Indus Valley civilization has not yet been deciphered? *T*

48. Around 2350 BC, which king of the Mesopotamian city of Akkad formed the first-known professional army and embarked upon the first-known wars of conquest, creating a Sumerian/Akkadian empire?

A Sargon I **B** Nebuchadnezzar **C** Hammurabi

49. From about 2200 to 1500 BC, the Sumerians built great temples on stepped towers. What were these known as?

50. In 2100 BC, what building was first raised in the Sumerian city-state of Ur, then rebuilt in the sixth century BC?

Ziggarat

51. What is the world's earliest story, written down in Mesopotamia around 2000 BC?

Gilgamesh

52. What cultural name is given to the people of Europe who made bell-shaped pots, often with horizontal bands of decoration, around 2000 BC?

Beaker People

53. Thought to have lived in the second millennium BC, which 'patriarch', originally from Ur in the Chaldees, Mesopotamia, made a covenant with God and founded the Jewish religion? He was also an important figure in the Christian and Muslim religions?

Abraham

54. King Hummurabi, who ruled Babylon from 1792 BC to 1750 BC, conquered the Sumerian/Akkadian empire, forging a strong state. What did he have inscribed on stone pillars and clay tablets?

Code of Law Hammurabi

55. The Great Pyramid of Giza at Cairo, Egypt, is the tomb of which pharaoh?

A Ramesses the Great **B** Cleopatra **C** Khufu

56. Which Egyptian pyramid is this?

A The Step Pyramid at Saqqara **B** The Round Pyramid in Hawara
C The Block Pyramid at Thebes

57. The Egyptian pyramids were originally covered with a smooth casing of different material to their basic building blocks. What colour and material was the casing?

A Red ochre **B** Green marble **C** White limestone

58. Sometime around 1700 BC, a lengthy climatic process finished changing the nature of a once fertile area in northern Africa. What is that area known as today? *Sahara desert*

59. Built between 1650 and 700 BC, Poverty Point in Mississippi is the largest and most complex earthwork of its period in North America. What is its most distinctive feature?

A A large circular mound **B** Beaten earth pyramids
C C-shaped, concentric ridges

60. What is this empire, which became powerful around 1600 BC, and was strong enough to invade Mesopotamia by following the Euphrates river, sacking Babylon in 1595?

A The Hurrite Empire **B** The Hittite Empire

C The Hackite Empire

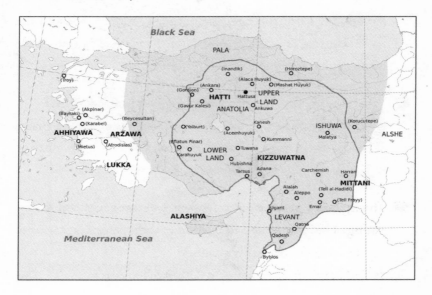

61. Where were the pyramids of Kush built?

A Egypt **B** Sudan **C** Mesoamerica

62. Between 1580 BC to 1080 BC, Egypt became a particularly dominant power in the Mediterranean and North African regions. Which two neighbouring countries did Egypt gain control of?

A Nubia and Palestine **B** Libya and Nubia **C** Libya and Palestine

63. Around 1500 BC, an early civilization in the Americas arose along the east coast of Mexico and the Gulf of Mexico. These people were known for building massive stone heads. Were they

A Toltecs **B** Olmecs **C** Aztecs?

64. Why is the period from around 1500 BC to 800 BC known in India as the Vedic Age? *Vedic Texts*

65. True or false? The 'oracle shells' from China during the Shang dynasty provide a unique record of society at the time. *T*

66. Around 1473 BC, the Egyptian queen regent Hatshepsut took control as sole pharaoh. True or false? From that date she was often depicted in man's clothing and wearing a false beard. *T*

67. What was the first recorded individual battle, in 1457 BC?
A The Battle of Jericho between the Israelites and the Canaanites
B The Battle of the Euphrates between Egyptians and Hittites
C The Battle of Megiddo between Egyptians and Kadesh

68. True or false? The ancient Egyptians had three forms of writing: hieroglyphics, demotic and hieratic. *T*

69. What writing material was commonly used by the ancient Egyptians? *Papyrus*

70. The Mycenean civilization in Greece is associated with which buildings?
A Pyramids **B** Palaces **C** Potteries

71. Sometime between 1380 BC and 550 BC, a chalk figure of an animal was cut into a hillside in England. What is it called and where is it? *Uffington White Horse*

72. From 1365 BC, which northern Mesopotamian kingdom became the dominant power in the Near East and expanded into a massive empire more powerful than the Egyptians and the Hittites? *Assyria*

73. These huge, winged, human-headed lions or bulls flanked the entrances to the royal palace in which Assyrian city? *Nimrud*

74. Which Egyptian pharaoh, who died around 1335 BC, was later known as the 'heretic', since he ended polytheism and instituted the worship of just one god, the sun god, Aten?

75. What was the name of the Egyptian queen, wife of the heretic pharaoh, and what was the meaning of her name? *Nefartiti, beautiful woman*

76. What was the city that the heretic pharaoh built as his new capital? *Amarna*

77. Who was his son and successor? *Khamun Tutan*

78. Which Egyptian pharaoh is depicted here on a papyrus boat with an upraised harpoon, ready to strike? *Tut*

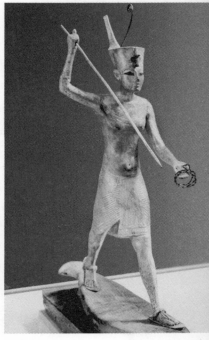

79. True or false? The world's first recorded peace treaty was made between Ramesses II (the Great) of Egypt and the Hittites. *T*

80. Which pharaoh had a temple built in his own honour at Abu Simbel? Known as the Great Temple, in 1964 it was painstakingly moved so that Lake Nasser could be created by the Aswan High Dam.

81. Around 1200 BC, a new, strong material was first used in central Turkey. What was it and what 'Age' did this start? *Iron Age*

82. In what modern country is the city where the Trojan Horse was built, around 1200 BC? *Turkey*

83. For how many years was this city besieged by the ancient Greeks, only falling at the end because of this trick? *10*

84. What was the name of the woman whose elopement began this war? *Helen*

85. According to the poet Homer, one of the Greek kings at this siege spent ten years trying to get home again. What was his name? *Odysseus*

86. Who were the port-based people of the Mediterranean who flourished from around 1200 BC and were known as great sea-traders? It is possible they sailed as far as Cornwall in England to trade for tin? *Phoenicians*

87. During the Battle of the Delta in 1175 BC, Egyptian pharaoh Ramesses III stationed archers along the banks of the Nile and destroyed the fleet that had been raiding the Mediterranean coast for years. What were the raiders known as? *Sea peoples*
A Sea Beggars **B** Sea Peoples **C** Pirates of the Caribbean

88. What profession were these Egyptian workmen engaged in? *Scribes*

89. By 1000 BC, the San people of Africa's Kalahari Desert were producing lasting artworks. What material were they made on?
A Papyrus **B** Pottery **C** Rocks

90. Around 1000 BC, Ionian Greeks founded twelve cities along the coast of Asia Minor, linked together in the Ionian League. True or false? Members of the League would gather at a festival called the Panionia to worship at the Panionium Sanctuary.

91. What West African people, or at least their language, began to spread through central and southern Africa from around 1000 BC? **A** Urdu **B** Mutu **C** Bantu.

92. Around 1000 BC, which Biblical king, who founded an important bloodline, ruled in Israel?

93. What was the name of this king's son, who was held to be particularly wise?

94. Around 1100 BC, the Mycenean civilization collapsed and for about 300 years Greek culture became simple and insular. What is this period known as?
A The Greek Renaissance **B** The Greek Dark Age
C The Classical Greek period

95. Around 1000 BC, city-states such as Saba began to develop in southern Arabia, thriving on the lucrative spice trade between Asia, Africa and Europe. What commodities did they particularly trade in?
A Frankincense and myrrh **B** Salt and pepper **C** Oil and vinegar

96. In which modern country was the large ceremonial site of Chavin de Huantar, the centre of the Chavin culture that flourished from around 900 BC?

97. Which people founded the city-state of Carthage in 814 BC?

98. In what modern country was Carthage, and where did its empire stretch?

99. Name the Seven Wonders of the Ancient World.

100. Which of these Seven Wonders is the only one still surviving?

ANSWERS

1. The Neolithic or New Stone Age.

2. **B** Huts on stilts or piles.

3. Copper.

4. **C** River valleys.

5. **B** Large, sunken, circular plazas.

6. The silkworm, which produces silk.

7. **B** Maize, which is also known as corn.

8. **C** Iraq, basically between the Tigris and Euphrates rivers.

9. Llamas.

10. Yes, it is the most complex stone circle in the world and is the only one with trilithons – two upright stones capped by a horizontal lintel stone. It is also the only stone circle where mortise and tenon joints were used (for the lintels) and where tongue-and-groove joints linked the upright stones into a circle.

11. True, probably.

12. Ötzi the 'Iceman'. Europe's oldest naturally preserved mummy who lived in the late Neolithic.

13. Skin tattoos.

14. The wheel, or wheeled vehicles.

15. Cuneiform.

16. **A** Sirius.

17. **A** Kingdoms – The Old, Middle and New Kingdoms.

18. Intermediate periods.

19. On the morning of the winter solstice.

20. Skara Brae.

21. C The Golan Heights, Syria/Israel.

22. True.

23. Gold and silver.

24. B Camels.

25. B City-states.

26. Avebury in England.

27. Great house.

28. Menes/Narmer.

29. C Nineveh.

30. The Minoan civilization based on Crete and other islands in the Aegean Sea.

31. Leaping over the horns of a bull.

32. True.

33. Knossos on Crete.

34. Axes.

35. A Vessels.

36. The Shang

37. Carnac, Brittany, France.

38. True.

39. C Imhotep.

40. C Memphis.

41. Pakistan and India.

42. The Indus Valley civilization

43. **B** The Yellow Emperor.

44. Flush toilets.

45. True.

46. **B** The rivers dried up and could not sustain concentrated populations.

47. True.

48. **A** Sargon I.

49. Ziggurats.

50. The Great Ziggurat.

51. The Epic of Gilgamesh.

52. The Beaker people.

53. Abraham.

54. The first known extensive law code, known as the Code of Hammurabi.

55. **C** Khufu or Cheops (his Greek name).

56. **A** The Step Pyramid at Saqqara.

57. **C** White limestone.

58. The Sahara Desert.

59. **C** C-shaped concentric ridges 1.2 kilometres (three-quarters of a mile) across their outer diameter.

60. **B** The Hittite Empire.

61. **B** Sudan.

62. **A** Nubia to the south and Palestine to the east.

63. **B** Olmecs.

64. Because the Hindu texts known as the Vedas were composed.

65. True. They form an important collection of ancient Chinese writing.

66. True. This was probably to show that she was a true pharaoh.

67. **C** The Battle of Megiddo between Egyptians and Kadesh.

68. True. The hieroglyphic 'picture' script was used on buildings and monuments. Demotic was a handwriting script for ordinary texts and hieratic was used for religious writings.

69. Papyrus.

70. **B** Palaces.

71. The Uffington White Horse, Uffington, Oxfordshire, England.

72. Assyria.

73. Nimrud.

74. Akhenaten.

75. Nefertiti, which means 'a beautiful woman has come'.

76. Amarna.

77. Tutankhamun.

78. Tutankhamun.

79. True. It took place fifteen years after the inconclusive Battle of Qadesh (Kadesh) in 1275 BC.

80. Ramesses the Great.

81. Iron and the Iron Age.

82. Turkey.

83. Ten.

84. Helen of Troy.

85. Odysseus, or Ulysses, as the Romans called him.

86. The Phoenicians.

87. B Sea Peoples.

88. They are scribes.

89. C Rocks.

90. True.

91. C Bantu.

92. King David.

93. Solomon.

94. B The Greek Dark Age.

95. A Frankincense and myrrh.

96. Peru.

97. The Phoenicians.

98. Carthage was in Tunisia, and its empire stretched around North Africa, the Iberian coastline and some Mediterranean islands.

99. The Great Pyramid of Giza, Egypt; the Hanging Gardens of Babylon; the statue of Zeus at Olympia, Greece; the Temple of Artemis at Ephesus (in present-day Turkey); the Mausoleum at Halicarnassus (present-day Bodrum, Turkey); the Colossus of Rhodes; the lighthouse at Alexandria, Egypt.

100. The Great Pyramid of Giza.

CHAPTER 2

800 BC–AD 449

1. Around 800 BC, which people founded settlements on the Iberian coast?
   A Phoenicians **B** Philistines **C** Peloponnesians

2. In 776 BC, what competition was first recorded in Greece?

3. The year 753 BC is traditionally held to be the date of the founding of which classical European city?

4. From about 750 BC, Greek colonists began to settle around the Mediterranean. Where were some of their earliest colonies?
   A Southern Italy and Sicily **B** Spain **C** Morocco

5. In the eighth century BC, what lasting cultural feature, a representation of speech, did the Greeks adapt from an earlier Phoenician system? It became the root of many future systems in the Western world.

6. Tiglath-Pileser III of Assyria, who ruled from 745 to 727 BC, accidentally created a historical legacy covering thousands of years when he adopted a new alphabet from the conquered territory of Syria. This newly introduced alphabet was simpler than earlier Mesopotamian scripts, so not only were all documents from then on written in it, but also older records were re-written in it. What alphabet was it? Its language was the ancestor of that spoken by Jesus Christ, along with people throughout the Middle East and Arabia.

7. Instead of counting using base 10, the Babylonians used base 60. So, instead of counting in single units up to ten, then multiples of ten up to 100 etc., they counted in single units up to 60. Has this survived to the present day?

8. True or false? From around 715 BC to about 645 BC, Egypt was ruled by a dynasty from Sudan (Nubia).

9. In 621 BC, an Athenian named Draco prepared an extremely strict code of laws. What adjective did he give his name to?

10. True or false? Around 600 BC, the Egyptian pharaoh Necho commissioned an expedition of Phoenicians to sail down the Red Sea and around the coast of Africa.

11. In 597 BC, which Babylonian king (pictured) conquered Judea and took the Jewish people into captivity in Babylon?

12. In 559 BC, Cyrus the Great founded the Achaemenid Empire in the Middle East. What name is his empire also known by?

13. Who was the Indian prince who lived around the sixth century BC, who achieved enlightenment, and whose teachings are the foundations of a religion?

14. Who was the Chinese philosopher, living from around 551 BC to 479 BC, whose approach to political, family and social life dominated Chinese culture for centuries and also influenced the political systems of other Asian countries, such as Korea and Japan?

15. Which ancient empire is shown here at its greatest extent from about 522 BC to 486 BC?

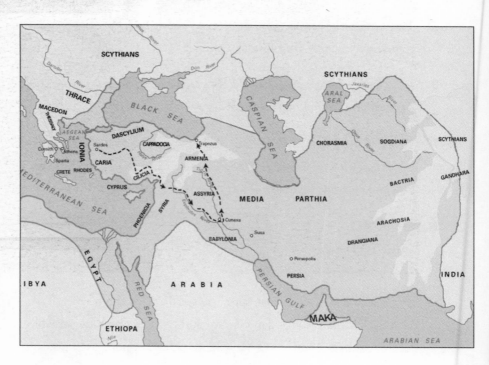

16. In 509 BC, after civil war in the kingdom of Rome, what form of government was established?

17. By 500 BC, Classical Greece had divided into several separate states. What name – a word that gave rise to the English word 'political' and its derivatives – is given to them?

18. Around 500 BC, the city-state of Athens developed a revolutionary new political concept. What was it?

19. Between 500 BC and AD 500, in what country were these lines made on the ground?

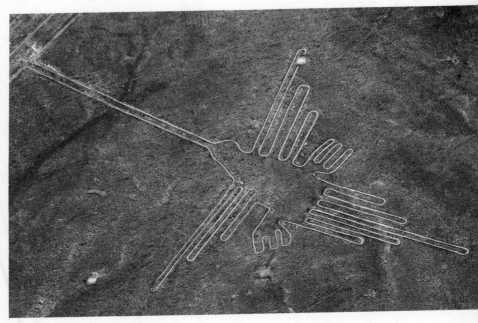

20. What book did the Chinese sage Lao Tzu write in the fifth century BC that inspired a philosophy known as The Way, which recommends accepting the way that change happens naturally in the universe?

21. Around 500 BC, Chinese people adopted a word for their state, implying that their country is the centre of the world, directly below heaven. What does this word, *Zhongguo*, translate as?
A The Middle Kingdom **B** The Blessed Kingdom
C The Holy Kingdom

22. From about 500 BC to AD 200, which culture, centred in present-day Nigeria, produced these stylized ceramic figures (right), the first known sculptures in Sub-Saharan Africa?
A Nok. **B** Swahili
C Benin

23. In 490 BC, what happened after a battle between Persians and mainly Athenian Greeks on a plain in Greece?

24. How many Spartans made a last stand against the Persians at the Battle of Thermopylae in 480 BC?

25. Who is this person (right), who lived in prehistoric Denmark?

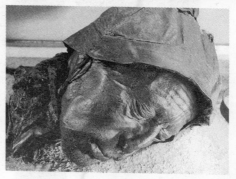

26. Although there were earlier chronologists, which Greek author, born in 484 BC, attempted to verify second-hand accounts and wrote the first critical history books, simply known as *The Histories*?

27. Which Greek author, born c. 460 BC, wrote *The History of the Peloponnesian War*, the first history book that did not assume a role by the gods in human affairs?

28. In 458 and 439 BC, Cincinnatus was appointed temporary dictator of Rome to deal with emergencies. After each crisis, he returned to his normal job, instead of trying to seize power permanently. What was he?
A A zookeeper **B** A farmer **C** A road-builder

29. Which two states (and their allies) fought the Peloponnesian War from 431 BC to 404 BC?

30. In 429 BC, a complex of buildings was completed on a huge rock overlooking a city in Greece. What is the name of this rock and where is it?

31. What and where is this city that was partly built into sandstone cliffs around 400 BC?

32. During an attack on Rome by Gallic tribes in 390 BC, Rome was saved by the warning noise made by which startled animals?
A Geese **B** Cows **C** Dogs

33. Which ancient Greek philosopher/scientist tutored Alexander the Great?   *Aristotle*

34. Who was the last of the Persian Achaemenid emperors, killed in 330 BC?
A Denzil I **B** Darren II **C** Darius III

35. Alexander the Great conquered so much territory that he is credited with introducing Hellenism, or Greek culture, across a wide swathe of the world. Where did this empire stretch from and to?
A Malta to Afghanistan **B** Crete to Alaska
C Gibraltar to the Punjab

36. What port did Alexander the Great establish in 332 BC when he conquered Egypt?   *Alexandria*

37. How old was Alexander the Great when he died in 323 BC?
A 22 **B** 32 **C** 42

38. Upon the death of Alexander the Great, his generals and friends divided his empire between themselves. Who took control of Egypt and founded a new Graeco-Egyptian dynasty?
A Ptolemy **B** Seleucis **C** Antigones

39. In 322 BC, Chandragupta Maurya began to forge which empire in India? It would become the first empire to rule nearly all of India, as well as other territory to the north-east and north-west?
A The Chandra Empire **B** The Gupta Empire
C The Maurya Empire

40. True or false? In ancient Greece, some states passed laws giving immunity to anyone who killed or attempted to kill a tyrant. Such assassins were known as tyrannicides. *True*

41. Which Greek state was famous for its harsh, military way of life? *Sparta*

42. What is this large, snake-like mound that was raised in what is now Ohio, USA around 300 BC? *Serpent Mound*

43. In 240 BC, Chinese astronomers made the first recorded observation of which comet? *Halleys Comet*

44. What animals did the Carthaginian general Hannibal take with him on his invasion of Rome in 218 BC? *Elephants*

45. During the second Punic War between Rome and Carthage, the Romans invaded the land of Lusitania in order to cut off Carthaginian access to the territory's rich metal sources. In which modern countries did Lusitania lie?

46. What was the final outcome of the Punic Wars? *Carthage totally destroyed*

47. In 221 BC, the king of a small, Chinese state completed his wars of conquest and established a new imperial dynasty in China, becoming known (wrongly) as the First Emperor of China, Shihuangdi. The name of his original kingdom is the root of the name China, and in its Arab version, is the root of 'Sinology' for the study of China. What was his kingdom called? *Ch'in*

48. Several small fortifications in China were strengthened and linked together in 214 BC to form what? *Great Wall*

49. What is the name of the Greek inventor (right), who was killed by invading Roman soldiers in about 212 BC, supposedly because he was so involved in a mathematics problem that he ignored their demands to come with them to their general? Clue: he is associated with a bath. *Archimedes*

50. Shihuangdi, the 'First Emperor' of China, built himself a magnificent tomb, ready for his death, which occurred in 210 BC. What formed a unique, massive feature of this tomb? *Terracotta Army* *Mound Tomb*

51. After the death of Shihuangdi, in 210 BC, there was a series of rebellions and power struggles before a farmer, Liu Bang, emerged triumphant and formed one of China's greatest dynasties. What was it? *Han Dynasty*

52. In 196 BC, the priests of Memphis in Egypt made this stone record of some temple transactions. What was the name of this stone, that eventually helped Egyptologists translate hieroglyphics? *Rosetta stone*

53. Which classical language was inscribed on this stone that helped decipher Egyptian hieroglyphics and why was it used in Egypt? *Greek : Demotic, Hieroglyphs*

54. Up until the reign of Emperor Wu of China (140–87 BC), government officials were simply appointed, regardless of ability. He made a significant change to the way that civil servants were selected. His innovation lasted for well over a thousand years. What was it? *Exams or University courses*

55. There were many centres of learning in the classical Mediterranean world. Where was the Great Library?
A Alexandria **B** Babylon **C** Corinth.

56. What were the three Servile Wars in Rome (135–132 BC, 104–100 BC and 73–71 BC)? *Slave Revolts*

57. Between 91 BC and 88 BC, several client states of Rome rebelled against it over issues of citizenship and unequal distribution of land. What is this war known as?

A The Neighbours' War **B** The Italian War **C** The Social War

58. From around 80 BC, the Roman Republic began to use the initials 'SPQR'. What did this stand for?

Senate & People of Rome

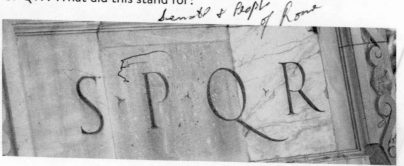

59. Between 78 BC and 6 BC, how did Rome make the Mediterranean Sea safe for travellers?

several campaigns wiped them out

60. In what modern country were Rome's Gallic Wars fought?

France

61. True or false? Julius Caesar was once captured by pirates and held to ransom. He was insulted by the low price the pirates asked for his freedom and insisted they should demand more money.

62. What action did Julius Caesar take against pirates?

pursued captured & crucified them

63. Who led the gladiators who organized a slave revolt against Rome in 73 BC, and what was the eventual fate of both him and his followers?

Spartacus crucified

64. Which empire, based in Iran, halted the expansion of the Roman Empire in the east by winning the Battle of Carrhae in 53 BC?

The Parthian's

65. What is this military tactic (right) that these people were famous for? *Parting shot (Parthian)*

66. Which Roman general conquered most of Gaul (France)? *Julius Caesar*

67. Which Roman general defied orders and marched his army across the Rubicon river towards Rome, saying, '*Alea jacta est*' or 'The die is cast'? *Julius Caesar*

68. True or false? The Romans founded the English city of London and the Scottish city of Glasgow, the French city of Paris, the German city of Berlin, and the Portuguese city of Lisbon. *F*

69. Julius Caesar was warned by a soothsayer to 'beware the Ides of March', a date on which he was indeed assassinated. What day of the month was the Roman Ides? *15 th*

70. Who formed the Second Roman Triumvirate in 43 BC?

A Romulus, Remus and Brutus

B Julius Caesar, Crassus and Pompey

C Octavian (Augustus), Mark Antony and Marcus Aemilius Lepidus

71. Who was the last ruler of the Ptolemaic dynasty of Egypt? *Cleopatra XII*

72. True or false? The leader of a coalition of local tribes, who defeated the Romans at the Teutoburg Forest in AD 9, driving the Roman Empire behind the Rhine river forever, was Hermann the German.

73. In AD 27, what title did Augustus adopt and what political system did Rome change to?

Emperor, Empire

74. Who was executed in Palestine around AD 33?

Jesus

75. Who was the Roman emperor at the time of this execution? *Tiberius*

76. Which Roman emperor appointed his horse as senator? *Caligula*

77. What does the name of this emperor mean? *Little Boots*

78. What was the name of the elite Roman military unit that, beginning with Claudius in AD 41, was powerful enough to acclaim individuals as emperor? *Praetorian Guard*

79. In AD 43, what country did Rome invade and begin to conquer? *Britain*

80. Who was this woman, who led the British revolt against Rome in AD 60? *Boudica*

81. Which two Roman cities were burnt to the ground by the rebellious Britons? *Colchester, London*

82. What was the Roman name for its province in north Africa? *Africa*

83. After a rebellion against Roman rule, which city was captured in AD 70 by the Roman general Titus, who destroyed its major religious site and began to exile the rebellious people? *Jerusalem*

84. Which volcano (below) erupted in September AD 79, and which two cities did it bury in ash and pumice? *Pompeii Herculaneum*

85. What common sign, found in translation today on gateposts and doors around the world, was discovered in the ruins of one of the Roman cities? *Cave Canem Beware of the Dog.*

86. Around AD 80, the Chinese princess, Douwan, died and was buried in an extravagant suit of a precious material. What nickname was she given after her grave was uncovered in the twentieth century?

87. True or false? Human sacrifice was legal in the Roman Empire until banned in AD 97. *T*

88. True or false? In AD 97, the Chinese envoy Gan Yin was sent to Rome but abandoned his journey at the Persian Gulf, when he was told by the Parthians of Iran that it would take two more years to reach Rome. *T*

89. What is this fortification, begun in AD 122? *Hadrian's Wall*

90. The Bar Kochba Revolt, between AD 132 and AD 135, was the last Jewish revolt against the Romans. What was its outcome?

A A victory for the Jews who pushed the Romans out of Judea

B A stalemate

C A victory for the Romans, who completed the Jewish Diaspora by sending Jewish people into exile from Judea

91. What is this city, whose popular queen, Zenobia, declared independence from Rome in AD 269 and began to take over parts of Rome's eastern provinces?

A Palmyra **B** Pandora **C** Pompeii

92. True or false? Zenobia's revolt against Rome was suppressed and her city was destroyed, but she married a Roman senator. *T*

93. The Persian prophet Mani, who founded the Manichean religion and died in AD 274, wrote that there were four great political powers in his world: China, Rome, Persia and where? *Aksum*

94. Where was these stone obelisks raised?
A Southern Egypt **B** Mesoamerica
C The kingdom of Aksum in Eritrea/Ethiopia

95. When and where did the large, two-tined cooking fork become adapted to the smaller, personal eating implement?
A Around 100 BC in China
B First century AD in India
C Around the fourth century in the Byzantine Empire

96. Where did the Huns originate from?

A Mongolia **B** Siberia **C** Central Asia

97. In about AD 376, the Huns began to extend into surrounding regions. What knock-on effect did this expansion cause?

other Barbarians pushed into west put pressure on Rome

98. What does this map show in 395?

Roman Empire

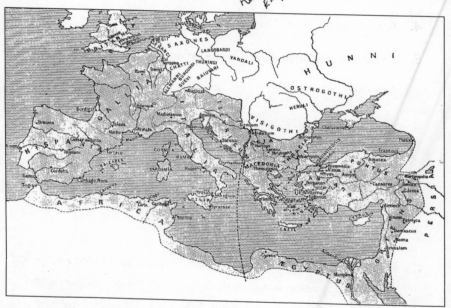

99. True or false? In 402, the capital of the Western Roman Empire was moved from Rome to Ravenna.

100. Who was the leader of the Visigoths who sacked Rome in AD 410? It was the first time in 800 years that the city fell to enemies.

ANSWERS

1. **A** Phoenicans.

2. The Olympic Games. Although a few competitions had taken place earlier, this is the first record of the Games.

3. Rome.

4. **A** Southern Italy and Sicily.

5. The first true alphabet with symbols for vowels as well as consonants.

6. Aramaic.

7. Yes. For example, we still count 60 seconds and 60 minutes of time and we divide a circle into degrees of 360 (six times 60).

8. True. The kingdom of Kush in Nubia (Sudan) conquered and ruled Egypt until driven south by an invasion of Assyrians.

9. Draconian, meaning severe and harsh.

10. True, according to a Greek historian who was particularly surprised that the expedition was able to circumnavigate Africa, since the Greeks at the time thought that Africa was linked by land to Asia.

11. Nebuchadnezzar II.

12. The First Persian Empire.

13. Siddhartha Gautama (Gautama Buddha or Buddha).

14. Confucius.

15. The Achaemenid or First Persian Empire.

16. Rome became a republic.

17. Polis.

18. Democracy – free votes for all participating citizens. At that time, women and slaves were excluded.

19. Peru.

20. The *Dao De Jing* or *Tao Te Ching*.

21. A The Middle Kingdom.

22. A Nok, named after the village in Nigeria where the ceramics were first discovered.

23. The Greek messenger Pheidippides ran about forty kilometres (nearly twenty-five miles) from the battlefield at Marathon to give the Athenians news of the Greek victory. He then dropped dead from exhaustion, but his run is commemorated in the modern marathon race.

24. Three hundred.

25. Tollund Man, one of the so-called 'bog bodies', whose body was naturally mummified and preserved by a peat bog.

26. Herodotus.

27. Thucydides.

28. B A farmer.

29. Athens (Delian League) and Sparta (Peloponnesian League).

30. The Acropolis in Athens.

31. Petra in Jordan.

32. A Geese.

33. Aristotle.

34. C Darius III.

35. C From Gibraltar to the Punjab.

36. Alexandria.

37. B 32.

38. A Ptolemy.

39. C The Maurya Empire.

40. True.

41. Sparta.

42. The Great Serpent Mound.

43. Halley's Comet.

44. War elephants.

45. Portugal and Spain.

46. Rome destroyed the city of Carthage and created the province in Africa out of Carthaginian territory.

47. Qin or, in the older style of transliteration, Ch'in.

48. The Great Wall of China (its first phase).

49. Archimedes.

50. The Terracotta Army, more than 7,000 life-size terracotta statues of soldiers and horses.

51. The Han dynasty.

52. The Rosetta Stone.

53. Greek, because the Macedonian Greek warrior-king Alexander the Great had conquered Egypt in 323 BC.

54. Examinations. He set up a university that taught the required Confucian principles of government for the civil service and conducted fair exams.

55. A Alexandria.

56. Slave revolts.

57. C The Social War.

58. It stood for the Latin phrase *Senatus Populesque Romanus*, meaning 'The Senate and People of Rome'.

59. Rome conducted several campaigns against pirates, eventually wiping them out.

60. France.

61. True. It happened in 75 BC.

62. He raised a private army, attacked and caught the pirates who had captured him, and executed them by crucifixion.

63. Spartacus. He was killed in battle, and 6,000 of his followers were crucified along the Appian Way, from Rome to Capua.

64. The Parthian empire.

65. The Parthian shot – shooting an arrow backwards at an enemy from horseback.

66. Julius Caesar.

67. Julius Caesar.

68. False. They founded London, Paris and Lisbon, but not Glasgow or Berlin.

69. Either the 13th or 15th, depending on the phase of the moon. In March 44 BC, the year he was killed, it was the 15th.

70. C Octavian (Augustus), Mark Antony and Marcus Aemilius Lepidus. Julius Caesar, Crassus and Pompey formed the First Triumvirate in 60 BC.

71. Cleopatra.

72. True. His German name was Hermann, although he was known to the Romans by the Latinized version, Arminius.

73. He became emperor and Rome became an empire.

74. Jesus Christ.

75. Tiberius.

76. Caligula.

77. Little Boots.

78. The Praetorian Guard.

79. Britain.

80. Boudica (Boadicea) the queen of the Iceni people in eastern England.

81. Colchester and London.

82. Africa.

83. Jerusalem. Titus destroyed Solomon's Temple.

84. Mount Vesuvius, and the cities were Pompeii and Herculaneum.

85. *Cave canem* or 'Beware the dog'. It was found in the House of the Tragic Poet in Pompeii.

86. The Jade Princess, since her burial suit was made of 2,160 pieces of jade, sewn together with gold wire.

87. True.

88. True. The Parthians were possibly lying in order to protect their valuable role as middlemen in trade between China and the Roman Empire.

89. Hadrian's Wall in northern England.

90. C A victory for the Romans, who completed the Jewish Diaspora by sending Jewish people into exile from Judea.

91. A Palmyra in Syria.

92. True.

93. Aksum or Axum in northern Eritrea and Ethiopia. It had a strategic position on the maritime trade route between India and Rome.

94. C The kingdom of Aksum in Eritrea/Ethiopia.

95. C Around the fourth century in the Byzantine Empire, although they may have been used earlier in ancient Greece.

96. C Central Asia.

97. Groups such as the Goths, Vandals and Alans were forced to migrate south and west, encroaching on the Roman Empire.

98. The permanent division of the Roman Empire between East and West. There had been earlier administrative divisions, but from then on no emperor ruled both parts.

99. True.

100. King Alaric I.

CHAPTER 3

450–999

1. The Gupta Empire of India lasted from 320 to 550. Because of its arts, literature and trade links, what is this period known as in India? **A** The Golden Age **B** The Age of Peace **C** The Age of Terror.

2. Which nomadic invaders undermined the Gupta Empire of India?

3. From the first to the fifth centuries, nomadic invaders threatened most of the Eurasian civilizations: the Greeks, Western Romans, Persians, Indians and Chinese. Which civilization was the only one not to succumb?

4. Which Central American culture produced this written language, the only one on the continent before Europeans arrived that could represent every aspect of life and society. Clue: they also had a complex calendar.

5. Who was ruler of the Huns in Central and Eastern Europe?

6. This Hunnish leader attempted to conquer Gaul, crossing the Rhine in 451 and marching to Orleans. He was defeated at what battle?

7. What area became settled for the first time by people fleeing attacks by the Huns in Italy?
   A Florence **B** Venice **C** Milan

8. In which country did Attila die in 453? Its English name derives from the Huns.

9. True or false? The Hun women veiled their faces.

10. True or false? In 476, the last Western Roman Emperor, Romulus Augustulus, was deposed by the Germanic invader Odovacer, bringing about the 'Fall of Rome'.

11. True or false? The period after the fall of the Western Roman Empire is known in Europe as the Dark Ages because it became difficult to get tallow for candles.

12. After the fall of the Western Roman Empire, much of Europe was invaded by people that the Romans called 'barbarians'. Which group eventually dominated Portugal and Spain in 485?
   A The Huns **B** The Visigoths **C** The Vandals

13. What was the name of this kingdom, founded by Germanic people spreading out in Italy? They gradually became 'Romanized'.

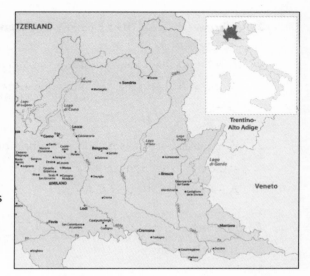

14. True or false? Vandals crossed into North Africa then attacked Italy from there.

15. Based in Hungary, where did the Avars attack from the fifth to the eighth centuries?

16. The Avars drove other people, the Slavs and the Lombards, into whose territories?

17. Where did the Slavs settle down?

18. The Byzantines continued to use Latin for 200 years, but which language eventually replaced it?
A Persian **B** Turkish **C** Greek.

19. About 495, an important Buddhist temple was built in Henan Province, China. It became associated with the development of Chan or Zen Buddhism, and (in legend), the development of Chinese martial arts. Much, much later, it inspired hundreds of kung fu films. What was its name?

20. Where did the Gaelic people known as Scots, who settled in what is now Scotland around the year 500, come from?

21. Between 481 and 511 a Frankish king united the Franks and extended their rule, defeating the Visigoths in southern France. What was his name and what dynasty did he belong to? His dynastic name was used much later in the Matrix movies and the background to *The Da Vinci Code*.

22. Which of these was not a Frankish king?
A Pepin the Short **B** Chlothar the Old **C** Trigo the Great

23. In the sixth century, Turkish people (speaking Turkic languages) moved south and west from which heartland?

24. This map shows the greatest extent of the Byzantine Empire. Which Byzantine emperor, ruling from 527 to 565, oversaw this expansion?
A Jason III **B** Julius **C** Justinian I

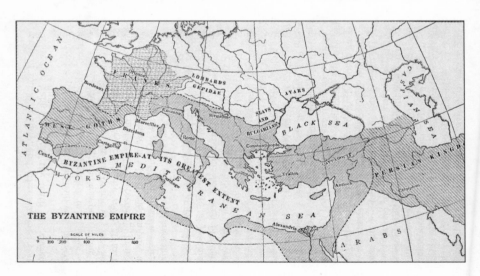

25. From 531, the prosperous Sassanian Persians invaded parts of the Byzantine Empire – Syria, Jerusalem, Anatolia and Egypt. Which Byzantine emperor forced them to retreat at Constantinople?
A Hercules **B** Herod **C** Heraclius

26. Both the Persians and the Byzantines soon then lost territories to which forces?

27. True or false? The maritime empire of Srivijaya in south-east Sumatra, that flourished from the seventh century, had important trade links with Bengal, the Islamic caliphate, and China.

28. In the late sixth century, the barbarian invaders of southern Europe began to convert to which religion?

29. Despite resisting invaders, China was fragmented by the constant incursions until the establishment of which dynasty in 589?
A Wei **B** Tang **C** Sui

30. During the time before reunification, Northern China fragmented and stopped using what helpful commercial aid?

31. Around 600, China introduced an early form of mass communication. Was it
A The telephone **B** The bicycle **C** Block printing?

32. What did the Arab merchant Muhammad receive in 610?

33. In 618, the Chinese aristocratic rebel Li Yuan founded a new dynasty that became renowned for its artistic developments. Later Chinese would look back on it as a 'Golden Age'. What dynasty was this?

34. When the prophet Muhammad died in 632, Muslims disagreed about who should be his successor as leader of the Islamic world. What enduring division did this disagreement eventually lead to?

35. During the 100 years after Muhammad's death, Arab Muslim armies conquered an empire as far east as the frontiers of China. What particularly helped their expansion?

A The transport systems that had been established on the Silk Road and by the Romans

B The areas they conquered had poorly equipped armies

C The neighbouring Persian and Byzantine empires had been weakened by war?

36. True or false? By 660, the Tang armies of China had conquered Northern Korea, parts of India, Central Asia, Afghanistan and eastern Persia. This took the Chinese Empire to its greatest extent before the reign of the Manchus in the 1700s.

37. After the first Muslim civil war in 661, which caliphate was established?

A Umayyad **B** Uthmanids **C** Sufyans.

38. In the seventh century, the Arab invaders of the Maghreb were resisted by which warrior queen?

A Hippolyta **B** Kahina (Dilya) **C** Boudica

39. In 696, the city of Venice in Italy appointed its first leader and chief magistrate. What title was given to this office?

40. From around 700, which culture built mounds like this one, Monks Mound, in the Cahokia Mounds, near Collinsville, Illinois, USA?

A Mississipian **B** Ohioan **C** Nevadan

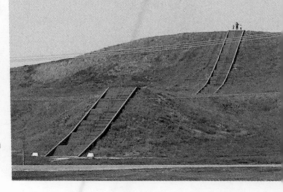

41. From 684 to 705, who was the only woman who ruled China as an empress in her own right?

42. From around 700, located in Chad, Nigeria, Libya and parts of Cameroon, which empire flourished?
A Danem **B** Ganem **C** Kanem.

43. In 711, most of Portugal and Spain were conquered by which people?

44. What name did the conquerors give to their new kingdom in Iberia?

45. In 732, the new regime in Spain invaded France, and was defeated at the Battle of Tours (Poitiers). Who led the Frankish forces that turned the invaders back?
A Charlemagne **B** Roland **C** Charles Martel

46. What was the Frankish system of inheritance, which eventually weakened their strength?

47. True or false? In 738, when the Arabs attempted to move eastward from Sindh, they were defeated by the Indian Pratihara Empire.

48. The battle of Talas River in 751 determined which culture would be the most influential in large parts of Central Asia. Which two powerful peoples fought there?
A Persians and Greeks **B** Indians and Russians
C The Muslim Abbasids and the Chinese

49. What was the result of the battle?

50. A seven-year rebellion from 755 resulted in Chinese withdrawal from which area?

51. Who instigated the rebellion?

52. How many people are thought to have died in this rebellion and the famine that followed the disruption to society?
A 1,300–3,600 **B** 13,000–36,000 **C** 13 million–36 million.

53. In 762, the Abbasid Arab caliphate established their capital city in present-day Iraq. What city was it?

54. Who was the Muslim Arab caliph (right) when the stories of the Arabian Nights or 1001 Nights were compiled in 786?
A Haroun al-Rashid
B Sinbad
C Omar Khayyam

55. In 793, what happened to the abbey of Lindisfarne in England?

56. Who finally destroyed the Avars?

57. True or false? In 791, the caliph of Baghdad presented Charlemagne with a camel and a clock.

58. On Christmas Day in the year 800, what happened to Charlemagne in the city of Rome (below)?

59. Why was Empress Irene of Byzantium infuriated by this?

60. By what names are the Frankish empire that Charlemagne founded known?

61. What social system, that lasted for centuries in Europe, did Charlemagne develop?

62. In 827, Muslims from North Africa seized which European island from the Byzantines?

63. True or false? The city of Dublin in Ireland was founded by Vikings in 841.

64. What name did the Vikings give to a law court?
A Moot **B** Court **C** Thing

65. Who took these routes from the eighth century to the twelfth century?

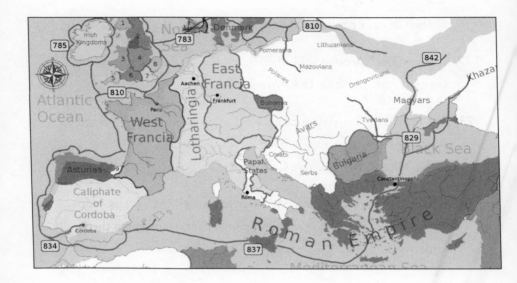

66. What is the name given to the medieval overland trader routes between China and the West?

67. What was the name of the military campaigns by Spanish and Portuguese Christians to reclaim land from the Arab and Berber states in Iberia?

68. By what name is Castilian military leader Rodrigo Díaz de Vivar, who fought against the Islamic states in Spain, usually known?

69. What empire, established around 400 and lasting until 1200, was located in south-eastern Mauritania and western Mali?
A Guinea **B** Ghana **C** Gibraltar Empire

70. This empire grew rich from the trans-Sahara trade in what commodities?

71. What city did the Yamato rulers of Japan model their capitals Nara (710) and Kyoto (794) on?
A Byzantium **B** Rome
C The Chinese capital at the time, Chang'an

72. True or false? Around 799, the Pacific Islands were populated by sea-going people from the Americas.

73. Around 800, the Mayan Empire in Central America weakened and the power vacuum was filled by which people?
A The Toltecs **B** The Incas **C** The Aztecs

74. In 843, three years after Charlemagne's death, his vast Frankish empire was divided into three kingdoms, centred in which three modern countries?

75. Where was the empire, known as the Khmer, that flourished from the ninth to the thirteenth centuries?

76. What was the capital of the Khmer Empire?
A Angkor **B** Byblos **C** Corinth

77. When the Khmer Empire began in 802, from whom did they gain independence?

78. The Khmer Empire first gained wealth through trade and agriculture, and was able to grow without resorting to what common means of expansion?

79. By 850, a small community of foreign merchants had settled in Kaifeng in China. Were they
A Italian **B** Jewish **C** Korean?

80. Who was the first in the line of Scottish monarchs? Clue: a Scot, he defeated the Picts, united most of the land known as the kingdom of Alba and died in 858.
A Kenneth Mac Alpin **B** William Wallace **C** Rory McRuidh

81. True or false? The name 'Russia' derives from the Arab name (Rus) for the Vikings who settled in the Baltic region from about 860.

82. Where in Britain did the Vikings establish a kingdom in 867?
A Edinburgh **B** York **C** Lincoln

83. The earliest known printed book, *The Diamond Sutra*, was produced in China containing the date 868. Was this
A A children's story **B** A list of emperors **C** A Buddhist text?

84. Which Anglo-Saxon king is the only monarch of England to be given the title 'the Great'?

85. During the Islamic Golden Age, a major centre of learning was established in Baghdad from the ninth to the thirteenth century. What was it called?

86. From the ninth until the thirteenth century, the Chola dynasty of south India ruled a large area of Southeast Asia, including Sri Lanka and parts of Malaysia and Indonesia. What helped them extend this way?
A They used war elephants
B They were the first Indian rulers to maintain a navy
C They starved out their enemies

87. Which people controlled the shaded dark area from about 650 to 965? They acted as a buffer state between the Byzantine Empire and northern nomads, the Sassanian Persian Empire and the Umayad Caliphate, and were eventually conquered by the Rus Vikings from Kiev.

88. Around 910, China experienced a shortage of copper so could not mint enough coins. As a result, what world-first did China introduce?

89. Which horsemen moved into Hungary in the late ninth century?
A Hagyars **B** Magyars **C** Hungyars

90. The Shia Fatimid caliphs, who controlled most of North Africa in the tenth century, took their name from
A Being very well-fed and fat **B** Their founder Fatah
C Descent from Fatimah, the daughter of Muhammad

91. In 929, Abd al-Rahman III declared himself the Islamic Caliph of the West. His capital city in Spain became one of the world's most important urban centres of the time, a place of learning and trade, where Christians and Jews could practise their religion and aspire to senior civil service positions. What city was this?

92. At the Battle of Lechfield in 955, Otto I (known as Otto the Great), Holy Roman Emperor, repulsed the Magyars. Why is this date significant for Europe?

93. What else is Otto renowned for?

94. Which strong king ruled Denmark from 958 to 986, countering the Germans and introducing Christianity?
A Harald Bluetooth **B** Harald Redtongue **C** Harald Yellowbeard

95. From around 960, where did a major Slav state arise, uniting several tribes in Eastern Europe?

96. In 969, what city did the Fatimid Caliphate found in Egypt as their new capital?

97. Why was Ethelred, king of the English, known as the Unready?

98. Who founded the first settlement on Greenland in 982?
A Erik the Red **B** Sweyn Forkbeard **C** Erik Erikson

99. True or false? From the tenth to the fourteenth centuries, the Varangian Guard, the elite bodyguard of the Byzantine emperors, was composed of British captives.

100. In 983, the Slavs of Eastern Europe halted the eastwards expansion of the Holy Roman Empire by uniting with which other people in the Great Slav Revolt?

ANSWERS

1. **A** The Golden Age.

2. Huns.

3. The Chinese.

4. The Maya.

5. Attila.

6. Battle of the Catalonian Plains.

7. **B** Venice.

8. Hungary.

9. True.

10. True. This was the end of the Western Roman Empire, which then fragmented into smaller states.

11. False. It is called the Dark Ages because so few writings were made (or survived).

12. **B** The Visigoths.

13. The Kingdom of the Lombards.

14. True.

15. Constantinople and Western Europe.

16. The Eastern Roman Empire.

17. Macedonia.

18. **C** Greek.

19. The Shaolin Temple.

20. Ireland.

21. Clovis of the Merovingian dynasty (descendants of Merovech).

22. **C** Trigo the Great.

23. Central Asia.

24. **C** Justinian I.

25. Heraclius.

26. The Muslim Arabs.

27. True.

28. Christianity.

29. **C** Sui.

30. Money. Bartering for goods was reinstated.

31. **C** Block printing.

32. Divine revelations that would become the Qu'ran, the holy book of Islam, whose adherents are Muslims.

33. The Tang.

34. The Sunni/Shia division.

35. **C** The neighbouring Persian and Byzantine empires had been weakened by war.

36. True.

37. **A** Umayyad.

38. **B** Kahina (Dilya).

39. Dogel .

40. **A** Mississipian.

41. Wu Zetian or Empress Wu.

42. **C** Kanem.

43. The Muslim Arabs and North African Berbers.

44. Al-Andalus, meaning the land of the Vandals.

45. C Charles Martel (Charles the Hammer).

46. Kingdoms were divided between all siblings.

47. True. Indian dynasties prevented the spread of the Arab Islamic empire further east.

48. C The Muslim Abbasids and the Chinese.

49. The Abbasids won and for 400 years Islamic rulers controlled Transoxiana, a strategic area between Asia and Western Europe. This facilitated the introduction of Islam to the Turkish peoples, and it is also believed that Chinese prisoners introduced paper-making to the Arab world and thence to Europe.

50. Central Asia.

51. An Lushan. He styled himself Emperor of Yan, but he was not able to take control of China.

52. C 13 million–36 million.

53. Baghdad.

54. A Haroun al-Rashid.

55. It experienced the first planned Viking raid on Britain.

56. The Frankish (French) king, Charlemagne – or Charles the Great.

57. False. Charlemagne was presented with a clock and an elephant named Abul-Abbas.

58. He was crowned Roman Emperor by Pope Leo III.

59. It meant that the pope and Charlemagne were not recognizing her legitimacy as Roman Emperor.

60. The Carolingian Empire, after the Latin version, Carolus, of Charles, his first name and that of his grandfather Charles Martel. Some historians also consider his empire to be the beginning of the Holy Roman Empire.

61. Feudalism.

62. Sicily.

63. True.

64. C Thing.

65. Viking raiders and traders.

66. The Silk Road.

67. The Reconquista or Reconquest.

68. El Cid (the Lord).

69. B The Ghana Empire, also known as Awkar.

70. Gold and salt.

71. C The Chinese capital at the time, Chang'an.

72. False, they were populated by sea-farers from Southeast Asia.

73. A The Toltecs.

74. France, Germany and Italy.

75. Cambodia.

76. A Angkor.

77. The Javanese.

78. Warfare.

79. B Jewish.

80. A Kenneth Mac Alpin.

81. True.

82. B York, the kingdom of Jorvik.

83. C A Buddhist text.

84. Alfred (ruled 871–99).

85. The House of Wisdom.

86. B They were the first Indian rulers to maintain a navy.

87. The semi-nomadic Khazars.

88. Paper currency.

89. B Magyars.

90. C Descent from Fatimah, the daughter of Muhammad.

91. Cordoba.

92. He unified the German tribes, and ended the Magyar invasions of Western Europe. This is seen as the beginning of the recovery of Europe from the Dark Ages.

93. His support for learning resulted in the Ottonian Renaissance.

94. A Harald Bluetooth.

95. Poland.

96. Cairo.

97. This doesn't mean that he was unprepared for events, but derives from the Old English word *unraed*, meaning 'bad counsel'. Reigning from 978–1013, he was only ten when he came to the throne, and was badly advised.

98. A Erik the Red.

99. False. The Varangian Guard was composed of volunteer Vikings.

100. Danes.

CHAPTER 4

1000–1399

1. Around the year 1000, what people founded a settlement at L'Anse aux Meadows in Newfoundland, Canada?

2. What is the name of this empire (right) that arose in southern India and had a great deal of influence in Southeastern Asia?

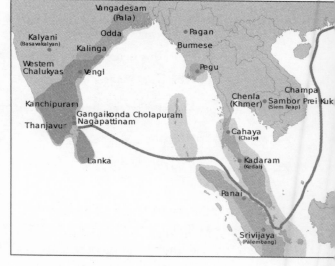

3. What name did the Vikings give to America?

4. From around 1000, what happened to many Italian cities?
   A They began to strengthen into city-states
   B They merged to form a powerful kingdom
   C They declined into weak villages

5. Who founded the Turkish-Persian Seljuk Empire in 1037?
A Seljuk Beg **B** Tughril Beg **C** Chagri Beg

6. In 1050, the King of Scotland made a pilgrimage to Rome. A strong, fair king, he was demonized by a great playwright many centuries later. What was his name?

7. After centuries of dispute about doctrine and politics, in 1054, the Christian churches based in Constantinople and Rome formally divided, excommunicating each other. What is this event known as?

8. What was 'danegeld', that was paid by many European countries to Norse raiders mainly from Denmark and Sweden?

9. Which battle is shown here that led to the conquest of a country?

10. Who was the Seljuk leader who met the Byzantine army at the Battle of Manzikert in eastern Anatolia in 1071?

11. What was the outcome of the Battle of Manzikert?
A The Byzantines strengthened their grip on central Asia
B It was a stalemate, leaving a power vacuum in central Asia
C The Seljuks won and gradually took Asia Minor away from the Byzantines

12. The Middle Ages saw many modern European countries emerge from the union of smaller states. Which important modern country had a different pattern at this time, with small, powerful, independent territories only loosely linked under an elected but fairly powerless king?

13. In 1086, the king of England instituted a survey of landowners and their possessions that has become a valuable historic record. What was it called and why?

14. True or false? The survey of land ownership in England was carried out in order to give to history a snapshot of English nobility.

15. In 1091, Vikings or Normans completed the conquest of which Mediterranean island, slowly creating a strong state including many mainland territories?
A Malta **B** Sardinia **C** Sicily

16. What empire is shown here (shaded dark) at its height in 1092?

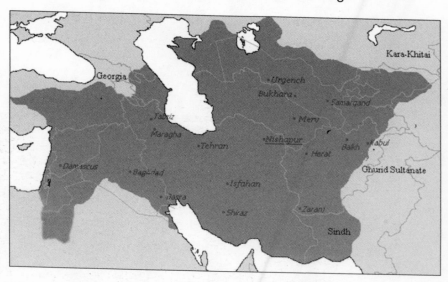

17. During the European Middle Ages, two types of monumental stone buildings developed. What were they?

18. Why did the Seljuk Turks choose the name 'the Sultanate of Rum' for their settlement in Asia Minor?

19. When Pope Urban II called for a Christian crusade in 1095, which empire was he hoping to aid?

20. Did the First Crusade of 1097–9 succeed in capturing Jerusalem?

21. What name did the Muslims defending Palestine give to all European crusaders, regardless of which country they came from?

22. From the eleventh to the fifteenth century, who built and occupied the city of Great Zimbabwe in the country now known as Zimbabwe?
A African peoples of the area **B** Arab traders
C Portuguese explorers

23. Which Central American culture is known for these reclining stone figures built in the eleventh and twelfth centuries in the former Mayan city of Chichen Itza?
A Aztecs **B** Incas **C** Toltecs

24. The reclining stone figures at Chichen Itza in Mexico all have a bowl on their stomachs. What do archaeologists think these were for?
A To hold offerings of food **B** To collect rainwater
C To hold the hearts of sacrificial victims

25. In the late eleventh century, the Nizari Muslim sect formed and took control of mountain strongholds in Persia and Syria. Their leader, Hassan-i-Sabbah, was known as 'the Old Man of the Mountain' and gave his name to their notorious activities. What was this group?

26. Approximately when did the era of building large stone statues begin on Easter Island in the Pacific Ocean?
A 1000 **B** 1100
C 1300

27. Which monastic order of knights was formally founded first, the Knights Templar or the Knights Hospitaller?

28. What was the purpose of both of these fighting Christian orders?

29. In 1126, which was the biggest country in Western Europe?

30. The cathedral of St. Denis in Paris, France, was built from 1130 to 1144 in a new architectural style. What was it?

31. Around 1132, the Chinese developed an explosively new military invention against Mongol raiders, bands of nomadic herdsmen and herders from the Mongolian and north Chinese plains. What was the new weapon?

32. In 1139, Prince Afonso Henriques, of the House of Burgundy, defeated the Spanish Muslims at the Battle of Ourique and became king of what independent country?

33. Who travelled along these routes in the Middle Ages?

34. The Second Crusade, from 1147 to 1149, failed to achieve any lasting victories in the Holy Land, but en route a group of crusaders helped which country expel Arabs from its major city?
A Turkey **B** Portugal **C** Syria

35. From 1154, this German king (right), Friedrich Barbarossa, attempted to extend German influence by campaigning against the Normans in Italy. Why was he nicknamed 'Barbarossa'?

36. In 1174, the bell tower of a cathedral in northern Italy was built. What is this building known as today?

37. Who is this Turkish leader (right), who captured Jerusalem in 1187, but prevented slaughter of the Christian inhabitants? He exchanged letters and gifts with Richard the Lionheart and went on to found his own Ayyubid dynasty.

38. The Third Crusade in 1189–92 failed to regain Jerusalem, but did win concessions for Christian pilgrims. Who were the main leaders of this crusade?

A Richard the Lionheart and Philip II of France

B Friedrich Barbarossa of Germany and Philip II of France

C Richard the Lionheart of England and Friedrich Barbarossa of Germany?

39. Was Richard the Lionheart King Richard I, II or III of England?

40. True or false? After he became king, Richard the Lionheart spent just one year in England.

41. In 1191, the third major order of crusading knights was confirmed by the pope. This order later campaigned against Slavs in Eastern Europe. What was its name?

42. In the twelfth century, a long-lasting dynastic struggle broke out between the houses of the Guelphs and the Ghibellines. Where did this struggle take place?

A Eastern Europe **B** India **C** Western and southern Europe

43. Richard the Lionheart of England embraced new military technology. He was killed in 1199 by what new weapon that he had urged his army to adopt?

A The cannon **B** The crossbow **C** The sling

44. In 1202, Leonardo Fibonacci of Pisa transformed European mathematics and even everyday life. What did he introduce?

A The concept of zero

B Arab numerals to replace Roman numerals **C** The abacus

45. In 1203, the Fourth Crusade set off from Europe to conquer the Holy Land from the Turks. Instead the crusaders were diverted to sack which Christian city?

46. Which Italian maritime city-state greatly benefited from the sack of this city?

47. Eleanor of Aquitaine, who died in 1204, married the kings of which two European countries?

48. In 1206, the scattered bands of Mongols in Mongolia and other nomadic tribes such as the Tatars united under Genghis Khan, a title meaning Great Ruler. What was his real name?

49. In 1209, the pope called for a crusade against heretics in Europe. Where did this take place?

50. What is King John of England doing in 1215 (right)? An unpopular ruler, he faced a near rebellion from his barons after he raised taxes, but to avoid civil war, he agreed to their demands.

51. What was the significance of this document?

52. Who were the main beneficiaries of this document?
A Serfs **B** Kings **C** Barons

53. In 1212, children from Europe formed their own crusade to try to capture Jerusalem from the Turks. What happened to the children?

54. Which Indian state repulsed Mongol raids from 1221 onwards and prevented the Mongol invasion of India?

55. True or false? The French king, Louis IX (reigned 1226–70), was the most powerful ruler in Europe and was later made a saint.

56. True or false? The descendants of King Louis IX ruled France until the French revolution in 1789.

57. In 1241, the mercantile towns of Lübeck and Hamburg in Germany formed a mutual defence pact to cover their trading ventures. This was the beginning of which powerful trading league of Northern Europe?

58. At its height, how many towns or guilds were members of this commercial league?
A 5 **B** 50 **C** 160

59. Under Genghis Khan the Mongols swept west, defeating the forces of Kiev, Poland, Romania, Silesia and Hungary. In 1242, why did they withdraw from pressing on into Europe?
A The Mongols were defeated in battle by the French
B The Mongols withdrew to elect a new Great Khan
C The Mongols were decimated by plague

60. The Mongols withdrew from Europe but left a lasting impact. They may have introduced gunpowder and they created a power vacuum in Russia. Which Russian duchy rose to power in their wake?
A Archangel **B** Moscow **C** Petrowski

61. The Knights Templar became extremely wealthy for several reasons. What financial facility did they offer to pilgrims that helped their wealth increase?

62. True or false? New Zealand was not permanently settled until about 1250 when Polynesians arrived.

63. From about 1250 to 1850 there was a significant climactic change in the Northern Hemisphere. Did the temperature get
A Warmer **B** Wetter **C** Colder?

64. In 1253, who won the Battle of Kosedag in eastern Anatolia, the Seljuks or the Mongols?

65. Following the Mongol attacks, what happened in Asia Minor?
A The Seljuk Sultanate of Rum expanded
B The Seljuk Sultanate of Rum was incorporated into the Mongol Empire
C The Seljuk Sultanate of Rum broke up into many small independent emirates

66. In 1250, Genghis Khan's grandson became leader of all the Mongols. What was he known as?

67. In what country did this Mongol khan establish his base?

68. In 1279, this Mongol khan completed the conquest of a large country, forming the first non-native imperial dynasty there. What was the country?

69. What was the name of the Mongol imperial dynasty in this country?

70. This map shows the Mongol Empire (in white) at its height around 1274. True or false? It was the largest contiguous land empire in history.

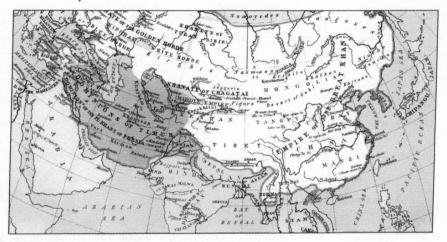

71. In 1271, who set out with a group of Italian merchants to travel along the Silk Road from Europe to China?

72. In 1271, Pope Gregory X received an unexpected letter of friendship from which powerful ruler?

73. In 1278, which family took control of Austria?

74. Around 1293, the Turkish leader Othman or Osman declared independence from the Seljuk Empire and began to build his own Islamic state in Asia Minor. What were his descendants known as?

75. In 1295, the 'Auld Alliance' was formed between Scotland and which other country?
A England B Wales C France.

76. According to legend, in 1306, the Scottish king Robert Bruce was on the run from the invading English and was on the point of despair, when he was inspired to carry on the fight. What inspired him?

77. Philip IV of France was heavily in debt and also hated a particular wealthy institution. In the hope of gaining some of its wealth, in 1307, he persuaded the pope to arrest members of the institution on suspicion of blasphemy. What group was arrested and eventually suppressed?

78. True or false? The Black Death contributed to the end of feudalism in Western Europe.

79. True or false? The St. John Ambulance Brigade is descended from the Knights Hospitaller.

80. Who were these dreaded creatures, who from the late Middle Ages in Europe were thought to bring all sorts of disasters, from famine to plague?

81. Between 1325 and 1354, another traveller journeyed along the Silk Road to China and later wrote his memoirs. This time he came from Morocco. Who was he?

A Omar Khayyam **B** Ibn Battuta **C** Ali Baba

82. Which Native American religion, developing around 1325, do these dolls belong to?
A The Sioux Ghost Dancers
B The Pueblo Kachina cult
C The Navaho Windtalkers

83. In 1327, which vassal of the King of France owned the largest territory in France?
A The King of England
B The Duke of Burgundy
C The Count of Amiens

84. A nephew of King Charles IV of France, who died without a son, this vassal believed he was the rightful heir to the throne of France. So when a cousin of Charles was crowned instead as Philip VI and then laid claim to personal holdings of the vassal, what did this vassal do?

85. True or false? The Hundred Years' War broke out in 1337 and saw more than 100 years of continuous conflict between England and France.

86. How many English kings ruled during the Hundred Years' War?
A Three B Five C Seven

87. How many French kings ruled during the Hundred Years' War?
A Three B Five C Seven

88. During the Hundred Years' War, who saved Orleans from a siege by the English?

89. What successive stages does this map show from 1347 onwards?

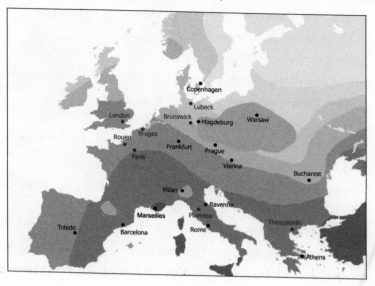

90. What was the Golden Bull of 1356?

A An icon worshipped in Poland

B A document specifying who could elect the German king

C A bull that survived many bull fights in Spain

91. Following a series of revolts in China, which new dynasty was established in 1368? It became famous for this type of porcelain vase.

92. True or false? In 1386, England and Portugal signed the Treaty of Windsor, the oldest formal alliance that is still in force.

93. In the European Middle Ages, people suffering from the contagious disease leprosy had to warn other people to stay clear of them. How were they supposed to do this?

94. What percentage of the total European population is thought to have died in the Black Death?
   A Ten per cent **B** Around forty per cent **C** Nearly fifty per cent

95. In 1377, there was an outbreak of plague in southern Europe. To try to prevent plague entering the city, Venice insisted that no one could disembark from visiting ships for forty days. What term did this edict give rise to?

96. Which countries fought the Battle of Kosovo in Europe in 1389?

97. What was the outcome of this battle?

98. In what European country did the Renaissance begin in the late fourteenth century?

99. What does the word 'Renaissance' literally mean and why was it applied to this period in Europe?

100. By the late Middle Ages the city-states in Italy varied from republics to kingdoms. What were the five most important states?

ANSWERS

1. Vikings, possibly under Erik the Red's son, Leif Eriksson.

2. The Chola Empire.

3. Vinland.

4. **A** They began to strengthen into city-states.

5. **B** Tughril Beg, grandson of Seljuk who gave his name to the dynasty.

6. Macbeth.

7. The Great Schism.

8. Effectively 'protection money'. The raiders were given money in order not to carry out attacks. The term is also applied to taxes raised for military purposes.

9. The Battle of Hastings, when William of Normandy began to conquer England.

10. Alp Arslan.

11. **C** The Seljuks won and gradually took Asia Minor away from the Byzantines, replacing the Greek influence in the area with their Turko-Muslim influence.

12. Germany.

13. Because it was such a complete listing of assets it came to be called the Domesday Book in reference to the Last Judgement of Doomsday, when a full record of an individual's deeds would be presented to God for judgement.

14. False. Its main purpose was to allow the king to assess taxes.

15. **C** Sicily.

16. The Seljuk Empire.

17. Castles and cathedrals.

18. 'Rum' derived from Rome and was used to give the impression that the Seljuks had inherited the power of the Roman Empire.

19. The Byzantine Empire, which was losing territory to the Seljuk Turks.

20. Yes, the crusaders set up the Kingdom of Jerusalem and three other states: Tripoli, Antioch and Edessa.

21. Franks, meaning French.

22. **A** African peoples of the area.

23. **C** Toltecs.

24. **C** To hold the hearts of sacrificial victims.

25. They were thought to be the original Assassins.

26. **B** 1100.

27. The Knights Hospitaller in 1113, based on an earlier group of monks who worked in a hospital in Jerusalem. The Templars were formed in 1119.

28. To care for and defend pilgrims to the Holy Land.

29. France.

30. Gothic.

31. Gunpowder-fuelled rockets.

32. Portugal.

33. European crusaders aiming to seize the Holy Land of Jerusalem from the Muslim Turks.

34. B Portugal, which took back Lisbon from the Arabs.

35. It is Italian for 'Redbeard' after his hair colour.

36. The Leaning Tower of Pisa.

37. Saladin.

38. A Richard the Lionheart of England and Philip II of France.

39. He was Richard I.

40. False, he spent around six months in the country.

41. The Teutonic Knights.

42. C Western and southern Europe.

43. B The crossbow.

44. B Arab numerals to replace Roman numerals. It was relatively easy to add or subtract using Roman numerals such as I, V, C, but the multiplication or division was extremely complicated. Arab numerals – 1, 2, 3, etc – made all calculations much easier.

45. Constantinople.

46. Venice, which gained three-eighths of the Byzantine Empire.

47. France (Louis XII) and England (Henry II).

48. Temujin.

49. Southern France against the Albigensians of Occitania.

50. He is pictured here signing the Magna Carta, or Great Charter.

51. It was the first document to state that everyone, even the monarch, is subject to the law, and that everyone has the right to justice.

52. C Barons.

53. Most died or were enslaved.

54. The Delhi Sultanate.

55. True. He was widely respected throughout Europe as a powerful but just king.

56. True.

57. The Hanse or Hanseatic League.

58. C 160.

59. B The Mongols withdrew to elect a new Great Khan, and from then on they focused their attention on other parts of the world.

60. B Moscow.

61. They offered a type of banking cheque whereby pilgrims could deposit money at one Templar 'preceptory' and receive a letter of credit, which could be cashed in on arrival in Jerusalem.

62. True.

63. C Colder. The period is known as the Little Ice Age.

64. The Mongols.

65. C The Seljuk Sultanate of Rum began to break up into many small independent emirates.

66. Kublai Khan.

67. The north of China.

68. China.

69. The Yuan, meaning 'Beginning'.

70. True. It stretched undivided from the China Sea to central Europe.

71. Marco Polo.

72. Emperor Kublai Khan of China.

73. The Habsburgs.

74. The Ottomans.

75. C France.

76. A spider that kept trying to spin a web until it at last succeeded.

77. The Templars.

78. True. So many people died the surviving landowners did not have enough workers to farm the fields, so land-use changed.

79. True.

80. Witches.

81. B Ibn Battuta.

82. B The Pueblo Kachina cult.

83. A The King of England, Edward III.

84. Edward III of England declared war as the rightful heir, and began the Hundred Years' War.

85. False. The period saw a series of separate conflicts rather than one, long, continuous war.

86. B Five.

87. B Five.

88. Joan of Arc.

89. The Black Death plague epidemic.

90. B A document specifying who could elect the German king.

91. The Ming, meaning 'Bright' or 'Illustrious'.

92. True. Since that date Portugal and England (later the United Kingdom) have never fought against each other.

93. By ringing a bell.

94. C Nearly fifty per cent (although some authorities believe it was up to sixty per cent).

95. Quarantine, named after the Italian for forty 'quaranta'.

96. The Ottoman empire under Murad I and Serbia under Lazar.

97. Both leaders died, both armies were decimated, but the Ottomans were able to proceed into the Balkans and encircle Byzantium.

98. Italy.

99. Renaissance means 'rebirth' and it was used to indicate the rebirth of classical knowledge and artistic styles.

100. The Papal States, the Republics of Venice and Florence, the Duchy of Milan and the Kingdom of Naples.

CHAPTER 5

1400–1599

1. In 1400, which Welsh prince led the last Welsh revolt against the English and eventually took control of most of Wales? He was unable to hold on to power and the English resumed authority over Wales.

2. In the early 1400s, which wealthy banking family began to dominate Florence?

3. In 1403, the Chinese capital was moved from Nanjing (Nanking), known as the Southern Capital, to a city in the north. What was the name of this Northern Capital?

4. Between 1403 and 1421, the Chinese admiral Zheng He led large naval expeditions exploring Southeast Asia, India, the Middle East and which other region?

5. What was the nickname of the fifteenth-century Portuguese prince Henry who sponsored exploration of the west coast of Africa?

6. True or false? Lithuania did not become Christian until 1413.

7. Which battle of the Hundred Years' War was this? In the end, the longbows of the English and Welsh destroyed the French army.

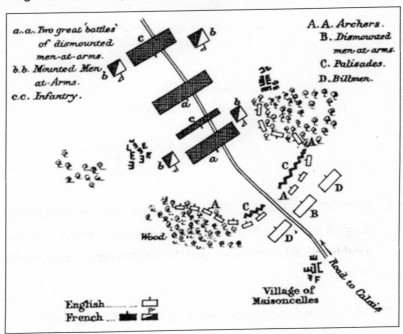

8. In 1415, Portugal captured which important North African trading centre as the beginning of the Portuguese Empire?
A Ceuta **B** Tangier **C** Marrakesh

9. What important invention in the late fifteenth century allowed the rapid dissemination of ideas throughout Europe?

10. Who is credited with this invention in Europe?

11. True or false? By the mid fifteenth century, France was a unified country.

12. Which major Christian city did the Ottoman Turks eventually capture in 1453?

13. What empire did this bring an end to?

14. The Venetians promised a large fleet to help this city fight the Ottomans in 1453, but what happened?
A It was unsuccessful **B** It failed to arrive **C** It was too late

15. True or false? The Ottomans succeeded in capturing this city due to the innovative use of gunpowder.

16. What effect did the Ottoman expansion in the Middle East have on world trade?

17. In around 1450 (or possibly earlier), the Iroquois Confederacy – or League of Five Nations – was formed to keep the peace between five tribes in the southern Great Lakes region of North America. The traditional founders were Deganawidah (the Great Peacemaker), and this man (below) about whom an epic poem was written. Who was this second peacemaker?

18. True or false? At the end of the Hundred Years' War in 1453, so many French nobles had died that the Crown was able to impose centralized control over the country.

19. What was the first European printed book, that appeared in 1455?

20. Between 1448 and his death in 1477, who was this warlord who was prince of Wallachia in Eastern Europe for three separate periods and gained a reputation for extreme cruelty, particularly because of the brutal form of execution he used?

21. Which fictional character is he thought to have inspired?

22. From 1455 to 1485, the Wars of the Roses were fought in England and Wales between which two families? And what colour roses did they adopt as their symbols?

23. Which king and dynasty emerged triumphant from the Wars of the Roses?

24. What is this powerful medieval European Duchy (shaded white, right) - and the areas it influenced – that was defeated by the forces of Lorraine and the Swiss Confederacy in 1477, and then absorbed by France?

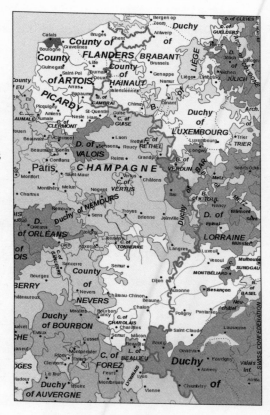

25. Muscovy, a north-east Russian territory, proclaimed independence from which people in 1480?
A The Cossacks
B The Fins **C** The Tatars

26. A dynastic dispute in Italy grew into the Great Italian Wars from 1494 to 1559 that involved most powerful European countries as well as nearly all Italian States. During the upheaval, Leonardo da Vinci moved from Italy to France. What painting did he take with him?

27. What was this empire (below shaded), which grew to become one of the largest in Africa? It was forged by Sunni Ali (1464–92).
A Madagascar **B** Ghana **C** The Songhai

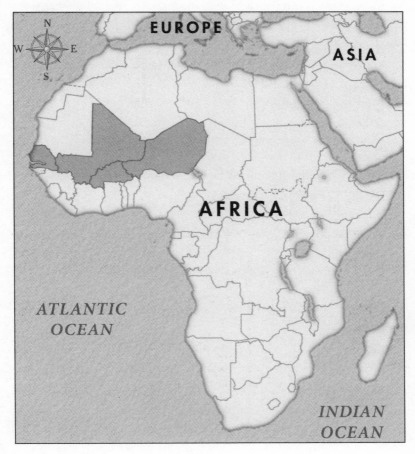

28. In the fifteenth and sixteenth centuries, one of the preeminent centres of Arab learning was an African city. Which one?

29. Why were the Baltics so important to Europe during this period?

30. In what year did Christopher Columbus set sail across the Atlantic from Europe and land in the 'New World'?

31. Which European monarchs sponsored Christopher Columbus's voyage of exploration that led him to the Americas?

32. What was the last Muslim Spanish kingdom, which fell in January 1492?

33. 1492 was a busy year for Spain. What did the Alhambra Decree (also known as the Edict of Expulsion) of March 1492 order?

34. In 1497, Portugal copied Spain and did what?

35. Which three ships were in Columbus's fleet in 1492?

36. When Columbus launched his expedition from Spain, what was he hoping to find?

37. Whereabouts in the Americas did Columbus make his first landfall?

38. Did Columbus ever set foot in North America?

39. Why did the Europeans call the indigenous populations of the Americas 'Indians'?

40. What is this line that was agreed at the Treaty of Tordesillas in 1494?

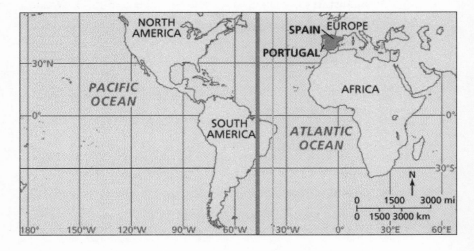

41. In 1497, John Cabot sighted 'Vinland' (Cape Breton in Nova Scotia, Canada) and claimed the land for which European nation?

42. In 1536, what lands did Jacques Cartier claim as 'New France'?

43. Who was the first European to reach India by sea in 1498?

44. This is considered a key event in world history. Why?

45. This expedition sailed around the coast of which continent to reach India?

46. Where in India did this expedition land?
A Bombay **B** Calicut **C** Delhi

47. The Swahili civilization on the east coast of Africa had a lucrative Indian Ocean trading complex. Where did Vasco da Gama arrive in 1498, beginning the European involvement in this and the Zimbabwe gold trade?
A Off the coast of Ethiopia **B** Off the coast of Somalia
C Off the coast of Tanzania

48. The German states expelled Jews between 1499 and 1553. Where did these Ashkenazim exiles mainly settle?

49. In 1500, the Portuguese explorer Pedro Cabral made landfall on the coast of South America and claimed the region for Portugal. What country is that now?

50. In the fifteenth and sixteenth centuries, members of which Italian family were accused of poisoning, incest, adultery, theft, corruption and many other crimes?

51. Where did the Sephardic people (Jews from Iberia) mainly settle?

52. From 1501, which dynasty ruled Persia, opposing the Ottomans both ideologically and militarily?

53. In 1501, who were taken to the Spanish colonies of Cuba and Hispaniola (Haiti)?

54. In 1511, Alfonso de Albuquerque conquered which state in the Malay Peninsula for Portugal?

55. This led to Portuguese domination of which trade?

56. In the early sixteenth century, Guru Nanak founded which religion in India?

57. In 1513, the Spaniard Juan Ponce de León sailed north from Puerto Rico in search of the 'fountain of youth' and discovered a region with a long chain of small islands. It was the Spanish Season of Flowers, the Easter season when he discovered it, so what name did he give to this territory?

58. What was the name of the Aztec capital city that became the site of Mexico City?
A Tenochtitlan **B** Teotihuaca **C** Tlalcala

59. In 1514, China was visited by the first Europeans to arrive by sea rather than by land. What nationality were they?

60. Where did these Europeans establish a trading post in China, eventually developing the base into an unofficial colony?

61. Throughout the Middle Ages, Jewish people in Western Europe were often confined to specific areas. In 1516 in Venice, Jews were forced to live in an area that gave its name to all these segregated districts and later on, was applied to slum areas. What part of Venice was this?

The Ghetto

62. Which empire, ruling Egypt and Syria from 1250 to 1517, was destroyed by the Ottomans?

Mamluk Sultanate

63. In 1517, where did the German priest Martin Luther nail up his list of protests against the Roman Catholic Church that started Protestantism?

Wittenburg

64. What is Ferdinand Magellan most famous for?

1st Circumnavigation of Earth

65. Which three European nations were the first to try and establish colonies in North America?

Spain France Holland

66. In 1581, Spain claimed the Pueblo area of North America. What did they name the territory?
A New Spain B New Madrid C New Mexico

67. In 1584, the English claimed an area of North America and named it Virginia (present-day North Carolina). Why did they choose this name?

68. Which British courtier, writer and adventurer sponsored the first, unsuccessful English settlements in North America at Roanoke in Virginia?

69. What is this empire (right, shaded white), founded in 1526 by Babur, who was a descendant of Timur (Tamurlane) and also of Genghis Khan, and who invaded north India from Afghanistan?

Mogul

70. After conquering Belgrade, much of Hungary and Rhodes, the Ottoman Sultan Suleiman the Magnificent besieged which European city in 1529, where he was baulked and had to turn back?

Vienna

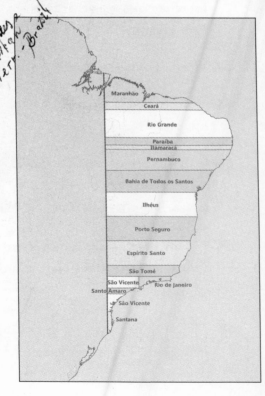

71. What does this map (right) show in 1534?

division of Amazon Fort. - Brazil

72. King Henry VIII of England was a younger son, who was not expected to become king. His older brother was given the name of a famous ancient king, a name that, because of the Tudor prince's tragic, early death has never since been used as a first name by the British Royal family. What was Henry's older brother called?

Arthur

73. In 1534, King Henry VIII of England broke from the Catholic Church and declared himself head of the Church of England. What was his main reason?

needed divorce Cath-Church rejected.

74. What was the English Reformation of 1536–40 also known as?

Dissolution of the Monasteries

75. What happened during the English Reformation?

76. Name the six wives of Henry VIII.

1 Katherine of Aragon   D Ann of Cleves   Anne Boleyn   K   Jane Seymour   CATHERINE Parr

77. What great state emerged in the 1500s, west of the Niger Delta, and was known for bronzes such as this (below)?

Timbaktu

78. Who was the last Aztec emperor in Mexico, who was killed by the Spanish conquistadors in 1520?

- Montezuma

79. Who was the last Incan emperor in Peru, who was killed by the Spanish conquistadors in 1533?

80. In the conquests of Mexico and Peru, what aided the Spanish victory?
A Existing divisions in the Aztec and Inca societies
B Larger armies
C Superior financial resources

81. Thousands of the Mayan people's bark-bound codices were destroyed by Spanish invaders. How many of these books survived?
A One **B** Four **C** Eighty

82. By 1560, what had become the chief export from the Americas to Spain?

83. What became the two most lucrative cash crops that Native Americans had already been growing before the European colonizations?

84. What important crop was introduced into Brazil and the Caribbean in the late sixteenth century?

85. Which Scottish monarch caused several scandals, particularly when she married the suspected murderer of her second husband in 1567? Forced to abdicate, she fled to England but was imprisoned and executed since she was a magnet for Catholic conspirators?

86. What was this 1571 naval victory by a Spanish-Papal-Venetian fleet over the Ottomans?

87. After the battle the Ottoman Grand Vizier said to a Venetian envoy: '. . . we have cut off one of your arms; . . . by defeating our navy you have only shaved off our beard. However, you know that a cut-off arm cannot be replaced but a shaved-off beard grows thicker.' What point was he making?

88. True or false? This was the last major engagement fought between rowing vessels in the Western world.

89. Which English monarch was on the throne when William Shakespeare's first play was performed?

90. Which country was the greatest sugar-producing territory from 1575 to 1600?

91. What did this economic opportunity cause a growth of?
A Dental caries **B** Emigration from Portugal **C** Bakers

92. True or false? In the sixteenth and seventeenth centuries Poland-Lithuania was one of the most densely populated and largest countries of Europe.

93. What did Pope Gregory XIII introduce in 1582? It is now the most widely used civil version around the world.

94. What was the name of the invasion fleet that Spain raised against England in 1588?

95. Sir Francis Drake was vice-admiral of the English fleet during the threat of the Spanish invasion in 1588. According to tradition, what did he insist on doing when the Spanish invasion fleet was sighted nearing England?

96. How was the Spanish invasion fleet defeated?

97. The Dutch flag is red, white and blue, so why do Dutch people wave orange flags or wear orange at national events?

98. True or false? Spain ruled Portugal from 1581 until a rebellion by the Duke of Braganza in 1640.

99. True or false? From the reign of Henry IV in 1594 until the end of Louis XV's reign in 1774, the French kings would have an official mistress, known as the *maîtresse-en-titre*.

100. What process revolutionized farming in Britain and the Low Countries, beginning in the sixteenth century, and leading to commercial farming?

ANSWERS

1. Owen Glendower.

2. The de Medicis.

3. Beijing (Peking).

4. Africa.

5. Henry the Navigator.

6. True. The process of Christianization only began in 1389. The last state, Samogitia, began to be Christianized in 1413; however this was only among nobles.

7. Agincourt.

8. **A** Ceuta.

9. Moveable type printing.

10. The German Johannes Gutenberg in 1438–9.

11. False. French unification was completed in 1589.

12. Constantinople.

13. The Byzantine or Eastern Roman Empire.

14. **C** It was too late.

15. True.

16. The Ottomans ended up in control both of the overland trading routes between East and West (the Silk Road) and the traditional sea routes through the Red Sea. As a result, Europeans found themselves cut off from the spices and other luxury goods of the

Far East. The need to find new sea routes to the East was one of the incentives behind the European Age of Discovery.

17. Hiawatha.

18. True.

19. The Bible.

20. Vlad the Impaler (Vlad Tepes).

21. The vampire Count Dracula. Dracula means 'son of the dragon' and was Vlad's patronymic, since his father was Vlad Dracul (Vlad the Dragon).

22. The House of Lancaster (red rose) and The House of York (white rose).

23. Henry VII, the first Tudor king.

24. The Duchy of Burgundy.

25. C The Tatars.

26. The *Mona Lisa*, which has remained in France ever since.

27. C The Songhai.

28. Timbuktu in present-day Mali.

29. They supplied the timber and supplies for shipping.

30. 1492.

31. Ferdinand and Isabella of Spain.

32. Grenada.

33. The expulsion of practising Jews from Spain.

34. Expelled Jewish people.

35. The *Nino*, the *Pinto* and the *Santa Maria*.

36. He was hoping to find a sea route to Asia to open up the spice trade.

37. The island of San Salvador in the Bahamas.

38. No. On future voyages he landed in Central America (Nicaragua, Panama and Costa Rica) and went no further than Honduras.

39. Christopher Columbus had been intending to find a sea route to Asia and he was convinced that the Caribbean islands he landed on were Asian, so he called the people 'Indios', Spanish for Indians.

40. The agreement by Spain and Portugal to divide discoveries in the New World between themselves along a North–South line 370 leagues (1,907 kilometres, or 1,185 miles) west of the Cape Verde Islands (about 46°30´ West). Spain was given rights west of the line and Portugal rights to the left of the line. Other European countries ignored the treaty.

41. England.

42. The region along the St. Lawrence river, Canada.

43. The Portuguese explorer Vasco de Gama.

44. It was the beginning of sea-based global trade and allowed for global imperialism in Asia.

45. Africa.

46. B Calicut.

47. C Off the coast of Tanzania.

48. Poland-Lithuania.

49. Brazil.

50. The Borgias.

51. In North Africa and the Ottoman Empire.

52. The Safavids.

53. The first African slaves to be taken to the Americas.

54. Malacca.

55. The spice trade.

56. Sikhism.

57. La Florida – 'land of flowers'.

58. A Tenochtitlan.

59. Portuguese.

60. Macau on the south coast.

61. The Ghetto.

62. The Mamluk Sultanate.

63. Wittenburg.

64. The first circumnavigation of the world, setting off from Spain in 1519. However, he did not complete the journey, being killed in the Philippines in 1521.

65. Spain, France and Britain.

66. C New Mexico.

67. It was named in honour of Queen Elizabeth I, the 'Virgin Queen'.

68. Sir Walter Raleigh.

69. The Mughal Empire.

70. Vienna.

71. The way that Portugal divided Brazil for colonization, in strips leading inland from the coast.

72. Arthur.

73. The pope refused to recognize Henry's divorce from his first wife.

74. The Dissolution of the Monasteries.

75. Henry VIII closed, sold or appropriated the wealth of religious institutions throughout England.

76. Catherine of Aragon, Anne Boleyn, Jane Seymour, Anne of Cleeves, Catherine Howard, Catherine Parr.

77. Benin.

78. Montezuma or Moctezuma II.

79. Atahualpa.

80. A Existing divisions in the Aztec and Inca societies.

81. B Four.

82. Silver.

83. Tobacco and cotton.

84. Cane sugar.

85. Mary, Queen of Scots.

86. The Battle of Lepanto, also known as the Battle of Three Empires.

87. The Ottomans had recently conquered Cyprus, and since the allied fleet had to return to their home ports, the Ottomans quickly rebuilt a navy and maintained dominance in the Mediterranean.

88. True.

89. Elizabeth I.

90. Brazil.

91. **B** Emigration from Portugal.

92. True.

93. The reformed Gregorian calendar.

94. The Spanish Armada.

95. Finishing his game of bowls on Plymouth Hoe.

96. By small English fireships and a storm.

97. A major leader of the Dutch Revolt against Spanish Habsburg rule, leading to Dutch independence in 1581, was William of Orange. The Dutch monarchy today is still the House of Orange-Nassau.

98. True.

99. True.

100. Crop rotation.

CHAPTER 6

1600–1799

1. By 1600, the arrival of Europeans in the Americas was already decimating Native American people, even those who had no contact with Europeans. Why was this?

2. During the seventeenth century, northern European companies established trade stations throughout which region?

3. Incorporated in 1602, which organization became the biggest trading corporation in Europe in 1619, establishing a monopoly in the valuable spice trade throughout the seventeenth century?

4. What does the Japanese title 'shogun' roughly translate as?
   A Military dictator **B** Benign ruler **C** Emperor

5. Who was the first shogun of the Japanese Shogunate period, which lasted from 1603 to 1867?

6. What is the period of the Tokugawa Shogunate known as?
   A The Time of Terror **B** The Perfect Kingdom **C** The Great Peace

7. In the early seventeenth century, the Ottomans were fighting two empires on different fronts. Who were these enemies?

8. In 1607, the first lasting English settlement in North America was established. What was the first settlement called, and why?

9. In 1613, Michael, the first of which dynasty, was elected tsar of Russia?

10. True or false? The earliest abolition of slavery in the Americas was in 1618, when the African former slave Gaspar Yanga was allowed to found a settlement of freed slaves in Yanga, Veracruz.

11. What was the name of the long-running war that devastated parts of central Europe between 1618 and 1648?

12. This war was precipitated by a political struggle in Prague that resulted in this clash of statesmen and windows. What is this event known as?

13. This war became a conflict between which two rival empires?

14. What aspect of warfare became particularly commonplace during this war?

15. Who were these colonists who arrived in North America in 1620 from Britain and settled at New Plymouth in what is now Massachusetts?

16. A year later, what did these settlers celebrate together with Native Americans?

17. In 1626, which island did the Dutch lease from Native Americans? They had a colony there named New Amsterdam.

18. In 1637, most Europeans were excluded from Japan. What was the only European nation that was still allowed to trade with Japan?

19. True or false? Under the Tokugawa Shogunate, Japan forbade its citizens from going abroad and banned the building of large ships.

20. Who was this French cardinal, who became the chief minister under Louis XIII? *Richelieu*

21. True or false? The victory in 1631 of the Swedish king Gustav Adolphus over the Holy Roman Empire at the Battle of Breitenfeld during the Thirty Years' War made Sweden a great power. *✓*

22. In 1632, what did the Indian Mughal emperor Shah Jahan commission in memory of his wife Mumtaz? *Taj Mahal*

23. In 1633, which Italian scientist recanted his scientific discoveries for fear of being burnt at the stake for heresey? *Galilee*

24. Due to the fur trade, the Russians reached deeper and deeper into Siberia, establishing forts such as Nerchinsk and eventually reaching which ocean in 1639? *The pacific*

25. This allowed Russia to control northern Asia and opened up what trade? *Silk Trade with China*

26. In 1643, there were about 100,000 eunuchs in the imperial service in China. How many of them served in the Forbidden City palace in Beijing?
A 10,000 **B** 50,000 **C** 70,000

27. In 1644, the second foreign dynasty seized control of China, naming itself the Qing (Ch'ing) meaning 'pure'. Who were these invaders and where did they come from? *Manchuria*

28. When these invaders of China took Beijing, what did the last Ming emperor do? *suicide*

29. Which kingdom is this (shaded white) that was part of the Holy Roman Empire, then part of the Austrian Habsburg Empire, then finally became part of Czechoslovakia? *Bohemia*

30. What name is given to the period from 1648 to 1715 when the French dominated European politics and culture, especially during the reign of Louis XIV? *The Grande Siècle*

31. In 1649, having lost the English Civil Wars, which king was beheaded? *Charles I*

32. Following the execution of the king, England entered a short period of republicanism. Who led the country with the title of Lord Protector? *Oliver Cromwell*

33. Where in Africa did the Dutch establish a settlement in 1652?

34. The Mughals extended their domains to the greatest extent under Aurangzeb (reigned 1658 to 1707) controlling nearly all of the Indian subcontinent. What did he commit in order to take power?
A Fratricide **B** Matricide **C** Patricide

35. In 1665, England captured the Dutch colony in North America. What new name was the colony given? *New York*

36. In 1666, London burnt down in the Great Fire. What beneficial impact did the fire have? *ended the Plague*

37. What was the Glorious Revolution in England in 1688?
A The Restoration of the monarchy
B The ascension of the Dutch Hanoverian William I and his wife Mary to the throne
C The formation of the rules of cricket

38. After clashes along the northern frontier of China in Manchuria, a peace treaty was agreed between China and Russia in 1689, the Treaty of Nerchinsk. The treaty set up boundary notices in Russian, Chinese, Mongolian and which other language?
A Latin **B** Portuguese **C** Urdu

39. Who was this seventeenth-century French king who was nicknamed the 'Sun King'?
A Louis XIII **B** Louis XIV **C** Louis XV

40. In 1682, where did the French king move his court to, compelling his nobles to also live there? *Versailles*

41. True or false? Although he was openly homosexual, Philippe, Duke of Orleans, a younger brother of the French Sun King, became known as the 'grandfather of Europe' since he did have children whose descendants are most of today's Roman Catholic European monarchs.

42. The Ottoman Turks again laid siege to Vienna in 1683. Who fought against them and won?

43. Which large territory changed hands as a result of victory over the Ottomans in that war?

44. In the late seventeenth century, the Chinese Qing dynasty embarked on a deliberate policy of maintaining the status quo in all areas of life, in order not to introduce changes that might trigger revolution. What lasting negative effect did this have?
A Chinese science and society stagnated, and for the first time China slipped behind Europe and Japan in industrial and technological development
B China began to re-adopt ancient customs
C Chinese scientists left the country for Japan

45. The first big gold rush in the Americas happened when gold was found in which country in 1693?
A Brazil **B** Canada **C** Mexico

46. Which seventeenth-century British scientist revolutionized the scientific view of the world and laid the foundations for science for centuries to come? Clue: according to legend he suffered a blow from an apple.

47. True or false? In 1697–98, Peter the Great of Russia worked supposedly incognito as a ship's carpenter during a visit to Western Europe.

48. During the seventeenth and eighteenth centuries there was a formal classification of race and mixed-race heritage that determined taxes and social status in Spanish-ruled countries in South America and Asia. What were the four racial categories in New Spain (the Spanish lands in the Americas)?

49. True or false? Only two formal racial classes could hold high offices in New Spain.

50. In 1700, Charles II of Spain died childless, ending which dynasty?

51. What nationality was the relative to whom he bequeathed his throne?
A French **B** Austrian **C** Portuguese

52. This resulted in the War of the Spanish Succession, when which three countries went to war to prevent this country from gaining more power and influence?

53. What was the eventual outcome of the War of the Spanish Succession?

54. True or false? The eighteenth century saw two other wars in Europe when the major powers objected to intended successions: the War of the Austrian Succession and the War of the Polish Succession.

55. What territory in the Mediterranean did Britain win from Spain in 1704? Clue: it has a population of wild monkeys.

56. In 1720, China absorbed which mountainous neighbouring country as a tributary?

57. Peter the Great of Russia defeated the powerful Swedish army at Poltava in 1709, acquired Estonia and Latvia in 1721, and founded St. Petersburg. Because of his achievements he was given what new title?

58. Peter the Great of Russia was keen to modernize the country, including adopting Western fashions. So in order to discourage old traditions, what did he place a tax on?
A Loincloths B Beards C Sheep-skull helmets

59. In the late seventeenth century, Chinese merchants began to make large profits from selling which commodity to European traders?

60. In seventeenth-century Britain, what were the 'Fifteen' and the 'Forty-five'?

61. What is the name of the French prince, bishop and diplomat, born in 1754, whose career spanned Louis XVI, the French Revolution, Napoleon, Louis XVIII and Louis-Philippe?
A Robespierre B Talleyrand C Marat

62. Which European city was practically destroyed by an earthquake and the subsequent tidal wave in 1755?

63. Suspicious of foreigners, in 1757 China restricted foreign trade to which port in the south?

64. This map shows the main European colonial claims in America around 1750. What countries do the numbers indicate?

NORTH AMERICA
1750.

65. In India, the Battle of Plassey (Palashi) in 1757 resulted in Bengal being annexed by the British East India Company. Who commanded the Company's forces?

66. What impact did the British victory in Plassey have?

67. In 1762, who organized a palace coup in Russia and went on to rule the empire with the epithet 'The Great'?

68. What were these outposts that Father Junipero Serra founded in California from 1768?

69. In the 1760s, what particular grievance did the British colonists hold against British rule?

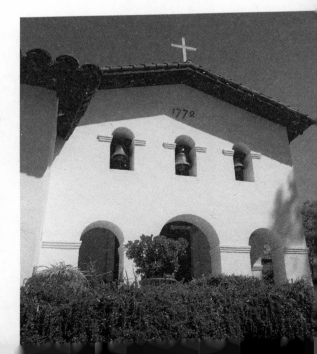

70. What was the name of the secret groups that developed among British colonists who were opposed to Britain's economic control?
A Daughters of the Glorious South
B Sons of Liberty **C** Children of America

71. Who claimed the east coast of Australia for the British in 1770?

72. When did the American Revolution or American War of Independence break out?
A 1774 **B** 1775 **C** 1776

73. Name the thirteen American colonies that declared independence in 1776 and founded the United States of America.
NH MASS RI CONN. N.Y PENN N.J. DEL
MARYLAND, VIRBINIA NC/SC GEORGIA

74. Who is this general and politician who was elected the first president of the USA? *Geo. Washington*

75. In 1777, which state became the first in Europe or the Americas to ban slavery?

A Britain **B** Portugal **C** Vermont

76. Who is this European monarch who in the late 1780s wrote a series of essays for an agricultural magazine under the name of Ralph Robinson? *George III*

77. What label is given to the first group of convicts who were transported to Australia from Britain in 1787–88? *The First Fleet*

78. In which country were totem poles important cultural items?

A New Zealand **B** Fiji **C** Canada

79. Who was the French monarch at the time of the French Revolution in 1789? *Louis XVI*

80. Who was his queen? *Marie Antoinette*

81. What event is shown here, that is generally held to mark the beginning of the French Revolution in 1789? *Storming of the Bastille*

82. What were the three classes or estates of French society before the revolution?

83. True or false? Before the French Revolution, most of the first and second estates did not pay taxes while the rest of the population (approximately ninety-seven per cent) did have to pay taxes along with feudal dues in some cases.

84. The French Revolution is considered a major event in modern world history, with global consequences. What were they?

85. What is the famous rallying cry originating from the French Revolution? *Liberté, Egalilé, Fraternité*

86. In the 1780s, trading vessels from Russia and Western Europe met on which coast, creating a global circuit of the fur trade?

87. In 1790, the Chinese Empire was at its greatest extent and its population was about 320 million. True or false? Its population was about twice that of the whole of Europe.

88. From the 1790s, British, French and American trading ships visited New Zealand. What other activity did they undertake in New Zealand waters?

89. What did the Maori of New Zealand trade huge amounts of flax, food and wood to Europeans for?
A Gold **B** Cotton **C** Muskets

90. What was the main cargo taken from Brazil to trade for slaves in Africa?
A Apples **B** Bananas **C** Tobacco

91. Where was the first successful slave rebellion in the Americas, from 1791 to 1804, that led to the establishment of a black republic?

92. Who led this slave rebellion?

93. By the late eighteenth century, Europeans had established plantations along the Atlantic coast from Brazil to Chesapeake, and in the Caribbean. Their main crops were cacao, tobacco, cotton, sugar and what other commodity?
A Oranges **B** Lemons **C** Indigo

94. Which European state became the first to pass a law banning the slave trade in 1792?
A Britain **B** Denmark **C** France

95. In 1793–94, Britain sent an embassy to China, hoping to gain trade and political concessions. What did the delegation's leader, Lord Macauley, refuse to do, leading to the failure of the mission?

96. In the late eighteenth century, European traders, predominantly British, began to illicitly sell which banned product in China?

97. This map shows the triangular slave-trading system. From which region of Africa did the majority of slaves come?

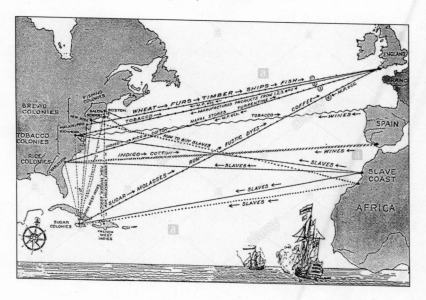

98. In the late eighteenth century, the slave trade reached its climax. In the last thirty years of the century, how many slaves were shipped from Africa?
A 1,300,000 **B** 2,300,000 **C** 4,300,000

99. Who took power in France as a military dictator in 1799?

100. In the eighteenth century, which country saw the birth of the Industrial Revolution?

ANSWERS

1. European diseases such as measles and smallpox, to which Native Americans had no built-up resistance, spread rapidly in advance of white colonization and killed thousands.

2. The Far East.

3. The Dutch East India Company.

4. Military dictator.

5. Tokugawa Ieyasu.

6. **C** The Great Peace.

7. The Safavids of Persia and the Habsburgs of Europe.

8. Jamestown, in honour of the then king of England, James I.

9. The Romanovs.

10. True.

11. The Thirty Years' War.

12. The Defenestration of Prague, when in 1618, four representatives of the king were thrown out of a window of Prague castle. This was actually the second Defenestration of Prague, since in 1419 seven city councillors were thrown out of the city hall windows by followers of the religious reformer Jan Hus (John Huss).

13. France and the Habsburgs.

14. The use of mercenaries, who looted indiscriminately or changed sides for more money.

15. The Pilgrim Fathers.

16. The first Thanksgiving feast.

17. Manhattan Island.

18. The Netherlands.

19. True.

20. Cardinal Richelieu.

21. True.

22. The Taj Mahal.

23. Galileo.

24. The Pacific.

25. The silk trade with China.

26. **C** 70,000.

27. They were Manchus from Manchuria, north of China.

28. Commit suicide.

29. Bohemia.

30. Le Grand Siècle (The Great Century).

31. Charles I.

32. Oliver Cromwell.

33. The Cape, South Africa.

34. **A** Fratricide.

35. New York.

36. It ended the plague that had broken out in 1665.

37. **B** The ascension of the Dutch Hanoverian William I and his wife Mary to the throne.

38. **A** Latin.

39. **B** Louis XIV.

40. The Palace of Versailles.

41. True. He had several children through two marriages.

42. Austrian, German and Polish forces led by the Polish king, John III Sobieski.

43. The Ottomans ceded to the Habsburgs most of Hungary.

44. A Chinese science and society stagnated, and for the first time China slipped behind Europe and Japan in industrial and technological developments.

45. A Brazil.

46. Isaac Newton, with his theory of gravity, laws of motion, calculus and other discoveries.

47. True.

48. Spaniards, born in Spain; Creoles, people of Spanish background born in the colonies; Mestizos, mixed Spanish and native background; Indians, the natives.

49. False. Only Spaniards could hold high offices.

50. The Spanish Habsburgs.

51. A French.

52. Britain, the Netherlands and Austria.

53. The huge Spanish Empire was divided but the balance of power in Europe was maintained.

54. True.

55. Gibraltar.

56. Tibet.

57. Emperor.

58. B Beards.

59. Tea.

60. The two Scottish Jacobite rebellions seeking to restore to the throne the deposed Catholic King James II and his descendants (such as the 'Young Pretender' Bonnie Prince Charlie). The rebellions began in 1715 and 1745.

61. B Talleyrand (Charles-Maurice de Talleyrand-Périgord, Prince de Bénévent).

62. Lisbon.

63. Guangzhou (Canton).

64. 1. Spain 2. France 3. Britain.

65. Clive of India (Robert Clive).

66. It was the beginning of British colonial control of India as the British East India Company realized it could conquer or dominate the smaller and weaker of the fractured Indian kingdoms.

67. Catherine.

68. Spanish religious missions.

69. Taxation without representation.

70. B Sons of Liberty.

71. Captain James Cook.

72. B 1775.

73. Connecticut, Delaware, Georgia, Maryland, Massachusetts, Pennsylvania, New Hampshire, New Jersey, New York, North Carolina, Rhode Island, South Carolina, Virginia.

74. George Washington.

75. C Vermont. It had become an independent sovereign state after the American Revolution.

76. King George III of Britain. His nickname was 'Farmer George'.

77. The First Fleet.

78. C Canada.

79. Louis XVI

80. Marie Antoinette of Austria.

81. The storming of the Bastille on 14 July 1789. A mob in Paris attacked the prison-fortress, the Bastille, to seize ammunition and to free political prisoners.

82. The clergy, the nobility, and everyone else.

83. True. The tax system and the privileges offered to the different classes caused a deeply unjust society.

84. The decline of absolute monarchies and the establishment of liberal democracies and republics.

85. *Liberté, Fraternité, Egalité* – Liberty, Fraternity, Equality.

86. Alaska.

87. True.

88. Whaling.

89. C Muskets.

90. C Tobacco.

91. Haiti.

92. Toussaint Louverture.

93. C Indigo.

94. B Denmark, although the actual institution of slavery was not abolished.

95. He refused to perform the kowtow to the Chinese emperor (kneeling and bowing the head to the floor).

96. Opium.

97. West central Africa, from where about thirty-three per cent of slaves were taken.

98. B 2,300,000.

99. Napoleon Bonaparte.

100. Britain.

CHAPTER 7

1800–1849

1. True or false? In 1800, the US bought the vast Louisiana Territory in North America from France.

2. In the early nineteenth century, why were British sailors nicknamed 'limeys'?
   A Many of them used to work in lime quarries
   B They were given lime juice to stave off scurvy
   C They were notorious for buying up limes in tropical ports

3. What was this area (not labeled, below) that the US bought from France in 1803?

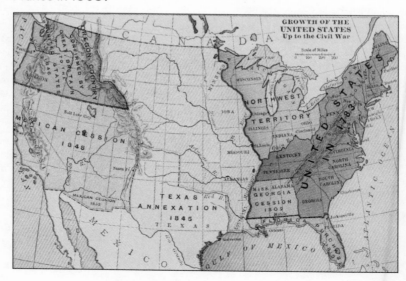

4. What was the name of the US expedition that made the first land journey from the east to the Pacific coast and back from 1804 to 1806?

5. In 1804, Napoleon took the new title of emperor. Who crowned him?
 A The pope **B** He crowned himself
 C A French girl chosen by ballot

6. Muhammad Ali, a commander of the Ottoman army, was made governor of Egypt in 1805. Because of his military, cultural and economic reforms, what is he known as?

7. Which British admiral died at the Battle of Trafalgar in 1805, in which Britain defeated the navies of Spain and France?

8. Although Britain ruled the waves between 1800 and 1809, Napoleon won decisive land battles against which three powerful European nations?

9. In 1805, who laid claim to the areas marked A?

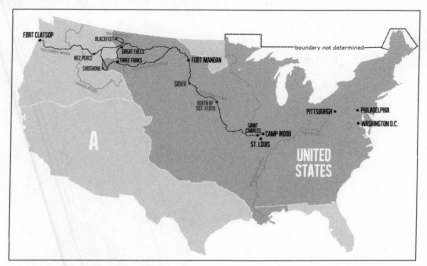

10. In 1807, the Napoleonic armies entered Portugal. Where did the Portuguese royal family flee to and establish a new capital?
A Brazil **B** Britain **C** Mozambique

11. In 1807, both Britain and the US passed laws banning what trade?

12. Napoleon also invaded Spain in 1808. Who did he install on the Spanish throne?

13. Napoleon's invasion of Iberia was fiercely resisted. What form of warfare was particularly widely used in this Peninsular War?

14. Who was this British general who came to prominence during the Peninsular War and commanded the Allied forces at Napoleon's final battle?

15. What was his nickname?

16. What item of clothing did he adapt and is named after him?

17. Between 1811 and 1812, British workers whose livelihoods were threatened by the new technology of the Industrial Revolution broke into factories in England and smashed up machinery. What are their protests known as?

18. In 1811, which country banned slavery, including in all its colonies.

19. During the war of 1812, fought between Britain and the US, which country did the US invade?

20. Where did the French unwisely invade in 1812?

21. Napoleon was the master of the pitched battle, but how did the Russians outwit him?

22. Who took this route in the winter of 1812?

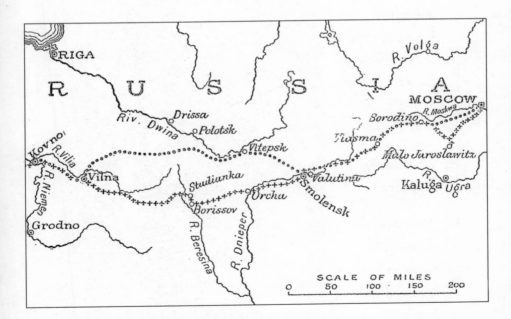

23. In 1813, European settlers found a route through the Blue Mountains west of Sydney in Australia. This allowed them to settle inland for the first time. Who led the expedition that found this route?

24. In 1814, an allied army of Russia, Austria and Prussia invaded France and took Paris, forcing Napoleon to abdicate. Where was he exiled to? A palindrome phrase that reads the same backwards as it does forwards, was later created as if said by him: 'Able was I 'ere I saw. . . '

25. Napoleon escaped and retook France. He was finally defeated by a British-led army at this battle (below). What was it?

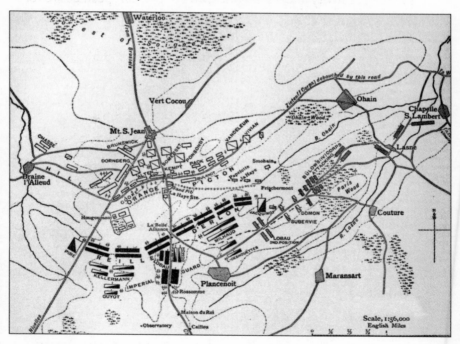

26. Who commanded the Prussian forces that helped defeat Napoleon in 1815?

27. To which remote island was Napoleon exiled, where he died at the age of 51?

28. Apart from military matters, Napoleon had a major influence on the development of the modern world. Why was this?

29. From 1800 to 1850, which two European nations saw the greatest emigration to the Americas?

30. True or false? Russia attempted to colonize North America in the nineteenth century.

31. In the early nineteenth century, the ivory trade was a major economic activity in central Africa, due to the European desire for ivory – for what purpose?

32. Much of the ivory trade in this period was conducted by which nation?

33. True or false? The ivory trade in East Africa was controlled by Arabs from Zanzibar, who raided areas around Tanganyika and Lake Nyasa for slaves at the same time.

34. What was the outcome of the Third Anglo-Maratha War in India (1817–18)?
    A It left Britain in control of much of India
    B It ended the Maratha Empire
    C It saw the Dutch East India Company strengthened

35. In the early nineteenth century, there were a series of Latin American revolutions aiming to achieve independence from Spain. There were several causes of this movement, but a particular trigger was Napoleon Bonaparte. Why was this?

36. Who was this Venezuelan-born revolutionary, who was called 'The Liberator' because of his efforts to achieve Latin American independence from Spain?
A Che Guevara
B Usain Bolt
C Simón Bolívar

37. What country is named after him?

38. In 1816, which Latin American country declared independence from Spain and, unlike earlier rebels, was not re-taken by Spain?
A Argentina **B** Brazil **C** Mexico

39. The other great figure of the Latin American Revolutions against Spain was José Francisco de San Martin. In 1817, he led his army across the Andes from the newly independent territory to liberate which country?

40. In 1819, The Liberator completed the liberation of the northern part of South America and formed Gran Colombia, a republic that he hoped would be an enlightened, liberal federation. Which modern South American countries was it originally composed of?

41. In 1820, San Martin moved his army north and helped Simón Bolívar liberate which Andean country?

42. What circle of latitude was used to mark most of the border between Canada and the US in 1818? The same line was later extended further west, although there were minor bumps in it to take account of geographical features.

43. In 1818 to 1819 in what is now the Eastern Cape, the Xhosa armies led by the prophet Nxele attacked the British in the Fifth Frontier War. Nxele was captured and imprisoned in which notorious prison?

44. In 1818, the US presidential residence in Washington D.C. was painted a distinctive colour. Because of this, what is the building known as?

45. In 1818, who began to forge a Zulu kingdom in southern Africa?

46. What impact did the rise of the Zulu kingdom have upon surrounding states?

47. In the 1819 Transcontinental Treaty, the US received Florida from Spain in return for giving up its claim on which territory?

48. True or false? By the 1820s, China experienced a trade deficit with Britain, even though British traders were importing about 23 million pounds of tea every year.

49. In Mexico, Agustín de Iturbide took control of Mexico City in 1821, gaining independence from Spain. By what title was he subsequently known?

50. In 1821, the American Colonization Society established a colony in West Africa for freed slaves. What country did this colony become?

51. True or false? In 1822, the Portuguese prince Dom Pedro declared independence for Mozambique and became its first emperor.

52. True or false? In 1823, the USA first expressed the Monroe Doctrine, which effectively threatened war with any European country that tried to interfere with a North or South American state.

53. In 1824, the US established the Bureau of Indian Affairs. What policy did it implement towards Native Americans?

54. During the Great Java War of 1825 to 1830, the Javanese people attempted and failed to wrest control of their country back from which European colonizer?

55. By 1825, the southern states of the US had become the world's largest exporter of which commodity? It was mainly grown and picked by slaves.

56. Where was this world-first public railway using steam locomotives that opened in 1825?

57. By 1826, all of Central and South America had achieved independence from Spain, apart from which two regions?

58. In 1826, members of the powerful, elitist Janissary army of the Ottoman Empire were up in arms when they heard that Sultan Mamud II intended to create a new, European-style army. What was the sultan's response?

A He backed down

B He turned cannon on their barracks and massacred them

C He offered a transitional period, with the Janissaries reforming themselves into the New Turk Army

59. In 1827, which country wrested independence from Brazil? |
A Mexico **B** Uruguay **C** Peru.

60. What name was given to the network of safe routes and safe houses used by runaway slaves in the US to escape to freedom in the northern free states or in Canada?

Underground Railroad

61. What name was given to the people who guided escaped slaves along sections of this safe network?

Conductors

62. Where was the first professional, full-time police force established in 1829?

A London **B** New York **C** Seoul

63. When did Britain annex the whole of Australia? *1829*

64. True or false? South-east Australia became extensively crop-farmed by British colonists. *F*

65. In 1830, Belgium won independence from which other European country? *Netherlands*

66. Having fought a war of independence in 1821, Greece was recognized as a sovereign kingdom in 1830. Ruled since the fourteenth century, from whom did they achieve independence?

Turkey – Ottoman Empire

67. Peaking in the 1830s, what did ships from Britain to Australia largely carry?

68. In which European country did the revolutionary secret society the Carbonari (charcoal burners) launch futile nationalist revolts in 1830–31?

69. Having worked together to achieve independence from Spain, from the 1830s many countries of which region sunk into wars between themselves, civil wars or coups?

70. In 1830, the French invaded what area of Africa, part of the Ottoman Empire?

71. In 1832, Muhammad Ali of Egypt established a seemingly forward-thinking institution, but because of a backward attitude in Egyptian society, who was allowed to use this new institution?

72. In 1832, who wrote: 'What experience and history teach us is this – that nations and governments have never learned anything from history, or acted upon any lessons that might have been drawn from it'?
A German philosopher Georg Wilhelm Friedrich Hegel
B American president Abraham Lincoln
C German philosopher Karl Marx

73. Which country abolished slavery in 1833?

74. True or false? When Britain abolished slavery, plantation owners in the West Indies were given £20 million in compensation.

75. Although trade unions were legal in Britain, what happened to six trade unionists from Dorset in 1834?

76. How many people signed a petition protesting about this?
A 100 **B** 1,000 **C** Nearly 800,000

77. In 1836, which territory revolted against Mexico to seek independence?

78. What is this building, site of a pivotal battle in March 1836, that was won by Mexico, but hardened the revolutionaries so that Mexico was decisively defeated one month later?

79. Who ascended to the British throne in 1837?

80. In the 1830s, a new long-distance communication device was introduced. What was it?

81. What was the Great Trek from 1835 to the early 1840s?

82. From 1837 to 1839, the Chinese government ordered that stocks of which commodity, owned by foreign traders, should be destroyed in the port of Guangzhou (Canton)?

83. In 1839, Britain sent warships to defend its merchants in China, beginning which war?

84. How many wars were there between Britain and China over this disputed commodity?

85. In order to stop pirate attacks in the Red Sea, which port in Yemen, formerly controlled by the Ottomans, did Britain occupy in 1839?

86. This port city became an important trading station for Britain. What crucial supplies were British ships able to pick up from there? **A** Salt and pepper **B** Whisky and cigars **C** Coal and water

87. In eastern Australia, the transportation of convicts ended in 1840. What discovery caused another wave of migration from Europe?

88. Having been thoroughly defeated by Britain in 1842, China was forced to make several concessions, including opening up more trading ports. Which island did China also have to cede to Britain?

89. Which natural resource was nineteenth-century industrialization dependent on? **A** Petrol **B** Coal **C** Wind power

90. During the nineteenth century, what major new transportation system allowed for the growth of industry?

91. In 1843, British colonists in the Natal found they had a labour shortage. Local Zulus, a warrior people, refused to work as labourers. Where did Britain turn to for workers?

92. True or false? Due to translation discrepancies, the 1840 Treaty of Waitangi, which was negotiated between Britain and Maori leaders and brought the North Island of New Zealand under British rule, is under dispute to this day.

93. In 1845, which crop failed in Ireland, leading to a disastrous famine and widespread emigration?

94. When was the 'Year of Revolutions' in Europe?

95. In 1848, the German revolutionary philosophers Karl Marx and Friedrich Engels published one of the most influential political books ever written. What was it?

96. In the early nineteenth century, what two processes, (indicated on this map), that went hand in hand, changed the way people lived in Western Europe?

97. In the early nineteenth century, which country was the leading manufacturer in the world?

98. By the 1840s, which country had developed the first national network of railways?

99. Instead of a range of local times, standardized time was first introduced in Britain in 1847 in order to synchronize which systems?

100. True or false? The conquest of Sindh and then Punjab in 1849 resulted in British rule of India's natural frontiers.

ANSWERS

1. False. Having been defeated by Napoleon Bonaparte, Spain was forced to cede the territory to France.

2. **B** They were given lime juice to stave off scurvy.

3. The Louisiana Territory. The exchange is known as the Louisiana Purchase.

4. The Lewis and Clark expedition or Corps of Discovery Expedition under Meriwether Lewis and William Clark.

5. He crowned himself.

6. The founder of modern Egypt.

7. Horatio Nelson.

8. Austria, Russia and Prussia.

9. Spain.

10. **A** Brazil, making Rio de Janeiro the new capital of the kingdom of Portugal.

11. The transatlantic slave trade – but not the actual institution of slavery.

12. His brother, Joseph.

13. Guerrilla warfare.

14. Arthur Wellesley, the Duke of Wellington.

15. The Iron Duke.

16. The Wellington boot. He asked his shoemaker to create slightly shorter riding boots that would better suit the new trousers of the time that replaced breeches.

17. The Luddite Riots.

18. Spain.

19. Canada.

20. Russia.

21. They mainly managed to avoid large-scale pitched battles by retreating in the face of his advance and operating a scorched-earth policy that eventually left Napoleon without supplies or winter equipment. This meant he had to retreat.

22. Napoleon's French army in its invasion and retreat from Russia.

23. Gregory Blaxland, William Lawson and William Charles Wentworth.

24. The Mediterranean island of Elba.

25. The Battle of Waterloo in 1815.

26. Field-Marshal Gebhard Leberecht von Blücher.

27. St. Helena in the South Atlantic Ocean.

28. He implemented some fundamental liberal policies, he instituted the legal Napoleonic Code, and he set up efficient civil administrations. All these would become widely copied, especially his Code that became the basis for legal systems around the world.

29. The United Kingdom (2.4 million) and Germany (1.1 million).

30. True. Russia built Fort Ross in California in 1812.

31. To make piano keys and billiard balls.

32. The Portuguese in Angola and Mozambique.

33. True.

34. A and **B**. It left Britain in control of much of India and ended the Maratha Empire.

35. In 1808, Napoleon invaded Spain and deposed King Ferdinand VII, putting Napoleon's brother Joseph on the throne. The Spanish colonials in Latin America did not think they owed any allegiance to Joseph, so decided to take control for themselves.

36. C Simón Bolívar.

37. Bolivia.

38. A Argentina.

39. Chile.

40. Colombia, Ecuador, Venezuela.

41. Peru.

42. The 49th parallel north or 49 degrees north.

43. Robben Island.

44. The White House.

45. Shaka Zula.

46. It caused immense upheaval, with the entire kingdom displaced or fighting others for territory. The time is known as the 'forced migration' or 'scattering'.

47. Texas.

48. True. So much opium was now smuggled into China by European traders that the balance of trade had shifted.

49. Emperor Agustín I.

50. Liberia.

51. False. He declared independence for Brazil and became the first Brazilian emperor.

52. True. The USA wanted to be able to exert its own influence on the continent.

53. 'Removal' – forcibly moving Native Americans to the west and out of lands that the white Americans wanted to settle in.

54. The Netherlands.

55. Cotton.

56. Between Stockton and Darlington in north-east England.

57. Cuba and Puerto Rica.

58. B He turned cannon on their barracks and massacred them.

59. B Uruguay.

60. The Underground Railroad.

61. Conductors.

62. A London.

63. 1829.

64. False. Demand for wool turned the area into a vast sheep farm.

65. The Netherlands.

66. The Ottoman Empire.

67. Convicts.

68. Italy.

69. Latin America.

70. Algeria.

71. He established a school of medicine for women, but because Egyptian society disapproved of the education of women, the first students were slave girls.

72. **A** George Wilhelm Friedrich Hegel in *Lectures on the Philosophy of History*.

73. Britain, although the ban was not enforced in some parts of the empire for many decades.

74. True.

75. Known as the Tolpuddle Martyrs, they were transported to Australia as convicts.

76. **C** Nearly 800,000. The Tolpuddle Martyrs were pardoned and released after three years.

77. Texas.

78. The Alamo mission near San Antonio, Texas.

79. Queen Victoria.

80. The telegraph.

81. The migration of about 12,000 Dutch-Boer settlers away from the British-controlled Cape Colony and further into South Africa.

82. Opium.

83. The First Opium War.

84. Two.

85. Aden.

86. C Coal and water.

87. Gold.

88. Hong Kong.

89. B Coal.

90. The railways.

91. India.

92. True.

93. Potatoes.

94. 1848, with revolutions in Italy, France, Germany, Austria and Hungary, none of which achieved any lasting change.

95. *The Communist Manifesto.*

96. Urbanization and industrialization.

97. Britain.

98. Britain.

99. The schedules of the various railway companies.

100. True.

CHAPTER 8

1850–1899

1. What name was given to the struggle for supremacy in Central Asia between Russia and Britain?

2. What did the Fugitive Slave Act of 1850 in the USA mean?
   A Escaped slaves became free the moment they stepped into a slave-free state
   B Escaped slaves had to be returned to their owners, even if they had reached a free state
   C Escaped slaves were given a grant to start a new life

3. True or false? In the 1850s, the American states Georgia, Mississippi and Texas banned the freeing of slaves.

4. The most devastating conflict of the nineteenth century was the Taiping Rebellion from 1851 to 1864, which led to the deaths of about 30 million people. In what country did this take place?
   A Russia B Japan C China

5. Under the Tokugawa Shogunate, Japan operated a strict policy of isolationism, refusing to trade with foreign nations. In 1853, United States Commodore Matthew Perry took his squadron into Tokyo harbour and demanded that Japan give the US a trade treaty. Japan did not have a navy, so what happened next?

6. What did Tsar Nicholas I of Russia describe in 1853 as 'the sick man of Europe'?

7. In 1853, the Crimean War was triggered when which country attacked the Ottoman Empire's fleet on the Black Sea?

8. True or false? Britain and France allied with the Ottomans in the Crimean War, partly in order to prevent territorial expansion by another country at the Ottomans' expense.

9. What event during the Crimean War is pictured here?

10. In 1853, the US set up army posts on the border with Canada. What effect did this have on the many Canadian First Nations, who were accustomed to following buffalo herds along the Prairies?

11. In 1855, vicious fighting broke out between the slave-owning and free factions in Kansas, USA, over disputed elections. What was this conflict known as?

A Dying Kansas **B** Bleeding Kansas **C** Broken Kansas

12. True or false? The American song 'John Brown's Body' commemorates an abolitionist who advocated armed revolt against slave-holding states and was hanged after leading a raid on slave-owners.

13. In 1856, Chinese officials seized a British ship at Guangzhou (Canton) under the pretext of searching for a banned substance. What conflict did this cause?

14. China was overwhelmed in the 1856–60 war with Britain and had to give concessions such as allowing foreigners to trade in several other areas and live in what became known as the Legation Quarter in Beijing. What indemnity was it forced to grant to Christian missionaries and Christian converts, a concession that caused great resentment and contributed to a later conflict?

15. True or false? The peace treaty that ended the British-Chinese war of 1856–60 was brokered by Russia, which won some territory for itself in the north of China.

16. What were the uprisings against British rule in India in 1857 known as?

A The Indian War **B** The Indian Revolt **C** The Indian Mutiny.

17. What changes to the government of India were made as a consequence of the Indian uprisings?

18. What was the Italian Risorgimento of the nineteenth century?

19. True or false? In 1859, the kingdom of Piedmont gave Nice and Savoy to France in return for French help to push the Austrians out of Italy.

20. In 1860, the Italian nationalist Guiseppe Garibaldi led a group of volunteers to fight against the foreign control in southern Italy. His army could not afford full uniforms, but managed to collect shirts of the same colour. Were they
A Black shirts **B** Brown shirts **C** Red shirts?

21. After a successful campaign against the Austrian troops occupying parts of Italy, as well as Garibaldi's expedition in the south and plebiscites in several provinces, what was founded in Italy in 1861?

22. Which important city was not yet part of it?

23. Which country defended the remaining Papal States in Italy?

24. True or false? After she staged a palace coup to become regent for her infant son Tongzhi in 1861, the Dowager Empress Cixi (Tzu-hsi) of China became the second female ruler of China

25. What social structure, that had been instituted in the Middle Ages, was abolished in Russia in 1861?
A The monarchy **B** Serfdom **C** The Catholic Church.

26. In 1862, who said, 'Not through speeches and majority decisions will the greatest questions of the day be decided . . . but by iron and blood'?
A The Prussian prime minister Otto von Bismarck
B The British Duke of Wellington
C The Italian Count Cavour

27. Who is this American politician, who was elected president in 1860, and what was his stance on slavery?

28. Seven slave-owning southern American states feared that the federal government elected in 1860 would ban slavery, so they left the Union in order to preserve what they believed was their states' right to continue slavery. In February 1861, they formed a new confederacy. Which states were they?

29. What was the first military action of the American Civil War?

   A The invasion of Washington D.C. by the Confederacy

   B The Confederate bombardment of Fort Sumter in Charleston harbour

   C The Union assault on New Orleans

30. Who was the general who eventually took overall command of the Northern Union forces and was determined to finish the war?

31. In 1862, who wrote, 'We cannot escape history'?

   A Danish philosopher, Søren Kierkegaard

   B French writer, Alexander Dumas

   C American writer, Mark Twain

32. Who commanded the Confederate Army of Northern Virginia during the American Civil War?

33. This is the final day of which important battle of the American Civil War, that saw the Union repulse the Confederate thrust into Pennsylvania in 1863?

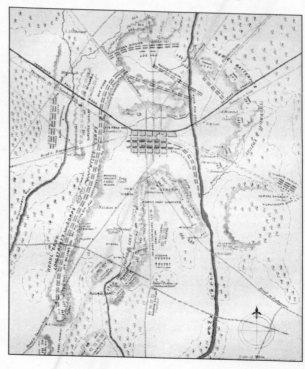

34. In 1864, during the American Civil War, who led the 'March to the Sea' or the Savannah Campaign through Georgia?

35. True or false? The first major action of the American Civil War took place partly in the farmhouse of Wilmer McLean. He moved to the village of Appomattox Court House in Virginia, away from the action. In April 1865, pursued by Ulysses E. Grant, Confederate forces under Robert E. Lee arrived there and chose McLean's house to carry out the official surrender.

36. What was the 13th Amendment to the US Constitution that became law in the US in 1865?

37. Who was assassinated at Ford's Theatre, Washington D.C. in 1865?

38. True or false? The American Civil War saw more American casualties – over 620,000 – than in any other war.

39. These American soldiers were known as Buffalo Soldiers. How did they get their name?

40. In 1867, what concession did the Austrian Empire make in the face of rising Hungarian nationalism?

41. Britain's 1867 Reform Act gave the right to vote to many more people than before, almost doubling the number of voters in England. How many extra men did the Act extend the vote to?
A 10,000 **B** 100,000 **C** 1,000,000

42. What did the British provinces of Quebec, Ontario, Nova Scotia and New Brunswick do in 1867?

43. Which territory did the USA buy from Russia in 1867?

44. In 1868, the Shogunate period in Japan ended and imperial rule resumed, modernizing Japan and opening the country to foreign influence. What was the new period called?
A The Meiji Restoration **B** The Samurai Revival
C The Tokyo Triumph

45. What event that linked the east and west coasts of the USA does this picture commemorate?

46. What was the surprise outcome of the 1870–71 Franco–Prussian War?

47. During the Franco–Prussian War, the French emperor Napoleon III was deposed and the Second Empire came to an end. A new French republic was declared. What number republic was it?

48. The Franco–Prussian War not only had a profound effect on both combatants, it also altered the development of Italy. How did this happen?

49. The prime minister of which German state led the drive for German unification, and what was his name and nickname?

50. True or false? This master politician gained extra territory for his state by manipulating Denmark, Austria and France into wars, which they then lost.

51. German unification was completed in 1871 and the German Empire was declared under Wilhelm I. What number reich (empire) was this?

52. Which red-coated, horse-riding police force was formed in 1873?

53. Just twenty years after the bloody and bitter hostilities of the Crimean War, the British and Russian royal families enjoyed friendly relations typified when the Russian royal family visited Britain in 1874. What brought about this new situation?

54. In 1875, Britain bought a share in an important new development in Egypt, and with the excuse of safeguarding it, gradually took over Egypt's infrastructure and administration. What was this development?
A The New Pyramid Company B The Suez Canal
C The Mummy Fuel Company

55. Who led the US troops at the Battle of the Little Bighorn in June 1876?

56. Who commanded the Native American forces at the Battle of the Little Bighorn?

57. Where was the Battle of Inkerman, which took place in the latter half of the nineteenth century?
A Germany **B** The Crimea **C** South Africa

58. What did Alexander Graham Bell demonstrate in 1876?

59. What new title was given to British Queen Victoria in 1877?

60. In 1877, the restored emperor in Japan began to reform society by removing some of the privileges of the warrior samurai, sparking a rebellion by some samurai. What was the rebellion called?
A The Mandarin Rebellion **B** The Orange Rebellion
C The Satsuma Rebellion

61. What happened to the rebellious samurai?

62. Who are these African people, who inflicted a rare defeat on British colonial forces at Isandlwana in 1879?

63. In 1881, what invention began to illuminate the western world?

64. In order to isolate France on the international stage, which other country formed the Triple Alliance with Austria and Italy in 1882?

65. True or false? Although the German philosopher Karl Marx, who died in 1883, was probably the most influential revolutionary ever, he never picked up a weapon apart from fighting a duel as a student.

66. What was the title of the Sudanese leader who led the 1883 uprising against Egyptian/British colonial rule?

67. In 1883, the US Supreme Court cancelled an earlier Civil Rights Act, and as a result an institutionalized form of racism was made legal. What was this?

68. How many assassination attempts did the British Queen Victoria survive?
A One **B** Five **C** Eight

69. True or false? In 1884, European countries met at a conference in Berlin to decide how they would divide Africa between themselves. Not one African nation was represented at the conference.

70. What is the name given to the European effort to colonize Africa from the 1880s onward?

71. True or false? When colonizing and dividing African countries, European nations paid no attention to existing borders or ethnicities.

72. What volcano is this that erupted in August 1883, affecting the climate and causing temperatures to drop all over the world?

73. True or false? In 1885, the North-West Rebellion by the Metis people in Saskatchewan, Canada, was suppressed within days because government forces used the new railways to quickly reach the area.

74. Who was this Apache leader (right), the last Native American warrior to surrender to the US army, which he did in 1886?

75. Which German inventor is considered to have built the first modern car in 1886?

76. This statue was installed in 1886. Where was it made?
A New York **B** Canada **C** France

77. Which British monarch was on the throne during the Jack the Ripper murders in London from 1888 to 1891?

78. Which South American country finally abolished slavery in 1888, the last country on the continent to do so?

79. In 1888, a European statesman predicted: 'One day the great European War will come out of some damned foolish thing in the Balkans.' Who was he?
A Otto von Bismarck **B** Winston Churchill
C Napoleon Bonaparte

80. True or false? In 1889, a military coup ended the empire of Brazil after the reigns of only two emperors.

81. In the USA, Native American resistance to the American government came to an end after which massacre in 1890?

82. In 1893, what was the first country to give all women the vote?

83. In the latter part of the nineteenth century, which European country began to gain control of parts of these countries, forming the Indochinese Union?
A The Netherlands
B Britain
C France

84. Which Chinese revolutionary was exiled in 1895? Like other exiles, as well as the few Chinese scholars who were allowed to study abroad, he absorbed more new or revolutionary ideas from the countries he lived in.

A Mao Zedong **B** Chiang Kai-shek **C** Sun Yat-sen

85. What did Pierre de Coubertin organize in Greece in 1896, a tradition that has continued every few years except for during the World Wars?

86. Which Chinese revolutionary was kidnapped by Chinese officials in London in 1896, but was freed after the British government intervened?

87. What is this African country, which Italy failed to conquer in 1896? It remained one of only two African nations not colonized or controlled by Europeans.

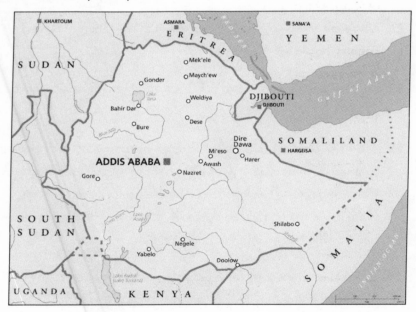

88. What was the other African nation that was not colonized?

89. In 1898, the USA annexed which island group in the Pacific Ocean?

90. The Spanish-American War of 1898 ended with the treaty of Paris that saw which islands, some in Southeast Asia, one in the Marianas group, and some in the Caribbean, handed over to the USA?

91. In 1898, Britain forced China to cede the islands around Hong Kong and agree a lease on Hong Kong for how many years?

92. In 1898, Cuba threw off Spanish rule only to come under the control of which other nation?

93. Who were the Boxers protesting about in the Chinese Boxer Rebellion of 1899–1901?

94. The Boxer Rebellion failed. What were the repercussions for the Chinese government?

95. After the Boxers besieged the foreign legation quarter of Beijing, an unprecedented alliance of eight nations was created to attack China and relieve the legations. The alliance included Austria, France, Germany, Italy and the UK, as well as which other three nations who had an interest in the region?

96. In the late nineteenth century, what name was given to the organized attacks on Jewish communities in Russia?

97. In 1899, colonization of the Pacific Islands resulted in Samoa being divided between the USA and which other country?
A Australia **B** Britain **C** Germany

98. True or false? The British Queen Victoria was the ancestor of six of today's European monarchs?

99. What country is this, the only country in Indochina or Southeast Asia to avoid being colonized or controlled by European nations?

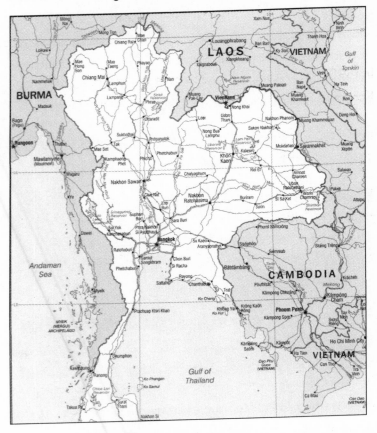

100. True or false? Queen Victoria ruled longer than any British monarch before her, sitting on the throne for 52 years.

ANSWERS

1. The Great Game.

2. **B** Escaped slaves had to be returned to their owners even if they had reached a free state.

3. True.

4. **C** China.

5. Japan realized that the US navy could enforce their demands, so gave in and opened two ports to US trade. This humiliation was followed when Britain, France, the Netherlands and Russia all used their navies to demand trading rights.

6. The Ottoman Empire, which was losing control of its Asian, North African and Balkan territories.

7. The Russian Empire.

8. True. Britain and France did not want Russia to increase its territory and therefore increase its influence, and they also wanted to protect their own spheres of influence.

9. The Charge of the Light Brigade, a unit of British light cavalry, which was given mistaken orders to charge a heavily defended Russian artillery position, and had to retreat with heavy losses.

10. They were all forbidden from entering the USA, meaning that they could no longer hunt buffalo all year round. Fighting broke out between previously peaceful tribes over shrinking resources.

11. **B** Bleeding Kansas.

12. True.

13. The Second Opium War.

14. Christian missionaries and converts were given indemnity from Chinese laws.

15. True.

16. **C** The Indian Mutiny.

17. The British East India Company lost the right to rule India, and the country came under the direct rule of Britain through a governor general.

18. The movement to unify the various Italian states and throw off foreign control.

19. True.

20. **C** Red Shirts.

21. The Kingdom of Italy.

22. Rome and the region around it formed the remainder of the Papal States and were not part of the new kingdom.

23. France.

24. True.

25. **B** Serfdom.

26. A The Prussian prime minister, Otto von Bismarck.

27. Abraham Lincoln, who was an abolitionist.

28. Alabama, Florida, Georgia, Louisiana, Mississippi, South Carolina and Texas. They were later joined by Arkansas, North Carolina, Tennessee and Virginia.

29. B The Confederate bombardment of Fort Sumter in Charleston harbour.

30. Ulysses S. Grant.

31. C American president, Abraham Lincoln.

32. Robert E. Lee.

33. Gettysburg.

34. Confederate General William Tecumseh Sherman. After capturing Atlanta in September 1864, his forces marched through Georgia to Savannah on the coast, causing chaos and destruction as they went. He then moved north.

35. True. Union officers then bought or stole several of the McLeans' furnishings as souvenirs of the surrender.

36. The abolition of slavery.

37. Abraham Lincoln.

38. True. More Americans died in the Civil War than in the Vietnamese War or either of the World Wars.

39. Buffalo Soldiers was the term given by Native Americans to the African-American troops of the US army that were formed in 1866 after the Civil War.

40. It became a dual monarchy as the Austro-Hungarian Empire.

41. C Nearly one million (938,000 to be precise).

42. Unite as a confederation, the Dominion of Canada.

43. Alaska.

44. A The Meiji Restoration.

45. The completion of the first transcontinental railroad.

46. France, still considered to be a dominant European military power, lost to the highly trained, larger Prussian army, signalling the arrival of a new power in Europe.

47. The Third Republic.

48. French troops that had been protecting the Papal States were withdrawn, allowing the Kingdom of Italy to annex them all, except for the Vatican, and complete the unification of Italy.

49. The Prussian prime minister, Otto von Bismarck.

50. True. He gained Schleswig from Denmark, Holstein from Austria, and Alsace Lorraine from France.

51. The Second Reich. The First Reich was the Holy Roman Empire.

52. The Canadian Mounties, or North-West Mounted Police.

53. Prince Albert (the future British King Edward VII) and Alexander, the heir to the Russian throne, had married sisters, the Danish princesses Alexandra and Dagmar, who sought to bring the families closer together.

54. B The Suez Canal.

55. Colonel George Armstrong Custer.

56. Sitting Bull.

57. The Crimea.

58. The telephone.

59. Empress of India.

60. C The Satsuma Rebellion, named after the province of Satsuma, where the samurai leader Saigō Takamori came from.

61. They were easily defeated by the imperial forces, who had been armed with modern weapons. The samurai leader and many others committed hari-kiri – ritual suicide.

62. The Zulus of southern Africa.

63. Electric lighting.

64. Germany.

65. True.

66. The Mahdi (religious leader).

67. Segregation, with separate public facilities for whites and blacks, especially schools. Those for African-Americans were nearly always inferior.

68. C Eight.

69. True.

70. The Scramble for Africa.

71. True. The divisions were often arbitrary.

72. Krakatoa in modern Indonesia.

73. True.

74. Geronimo (Goyalkla).

75. Karl Benz.

76. C France.

77. Queen Victoria.

78. Brazil.

79. A Otto von Bismarck.

80. True.

81. Wounded Knee in South Dakota.

82. New Zealand.

83. C France.

84. C Sun Yat-sen.

85. The first modern Olympic Games.

86. Sun Yat-sen.

87. Ethiopia (Abyssinia).

88. Liberia.

89. Hawaii.

90. The Philippines, Guam and the Puerto Rican archipelago.

91. Ninety-nine years, expiring at midnight on 30 June 1997.

92. The USA.

93. Western foreigners who were gaining influence in parts of China.

94. China had to pay crippling reparations to Western nations, a humiliating and economical problem that contributed to the future Chinese revolution.

95. Japan, Russia and the USA.

96. Pogroms.

97. C Germany.

98. False. She was the ancestor of only five European monarchs – those of Britain, Denmark, Norway, Spain and Sweden.

99. Thailand.

100. False. She ruled for sixty-three years and seven months, from June 1837 to January 1901.

CHAPTER 9

1900–1924

1. From around 1900 onwards, a revolutionary new theory changed physics. Was it
   A The Big Bang Theory **B** Quantum physics
   C Molecular chemistry?

2. Which of these countries was not part of the British Indian Empire in 1900? Nepal, Pakistan, Bangladesh, Burma (Myanmar), Ceylon (Sri Lanka).

3. In 1901, what did the six separate colonies in Australia do, and New Zealand decide not to do?

4. True or false? European military technology and air power meant that all rebellions by colonized Africans in the early part of the twentieth century were suppressed.

5. What was the name of the friendly alliance that Britain and France forged in 1904?
   A *Entente Amiable* **B** *Entente Ancien* **C** *Entente Cordiale*

6. What did Orville and Wilbur Wright do in 1902?

7. True or false? More than seventy-five per cent of the Herero population of German South-West Africa (modern Namibia) were killed as a result of their uprising from 1904 to 1907.

8. In 1904, who wrote, 'War makes rattling good history; but Peace is poor reading.'?
   A American president, Theodore Roosevelt
   B English writer, Thomas Hardy C Mahatma Gandhi.

9. On the night of the 21/22 October 1904 in what is known as the Dogger Bank Incident, the Russian navy fired on a British trawler fleet in the North Sea, killing three fishermen. Who did the Russians fear the fishing fleet was?
   A The British navy B The German navy C The Japanese navy

10. Which two Scandinavian countries formally separated in 1905?

11. In 1905, protests against the absolute monarchy by many different groups in Russia led to what is sometimes called the First Russian Revolution. The crew of which battleship mutinied and joined the protests?

12. What change to his absolutist monarchy did Tsar Nicholas II make in Russia as a response to the 1905 uprisings?

13. In 1905, a phrase that has been copied and changed several times was first written down: 'Those who cannot remember the past are condemned to repeat it.' Who wrote this?
   A Austrian psychoanalyst, Sigmund Freud
   B German physicist, Albert Einstein.
   C Spanish-American philosopher, George Santayana.

14. Who is this physicist, and why did he have what scientists call his *Annus Mirabilis*, or 'Miracle Year' in 1905?

15. True or false? In 1905, a revolution in Persia resulted in the country's first ever parliament and constitution.

16. True or false? Finland was the first European country to give women the vote in 1906.

17. In 1907, Britain and France were joined by which other country in the Triple Entente?

18. In 1907, Britain and Russia put a final end to their rivalry, 'the Great Game', in Central Asia by taking over which country and dividing it into separate spheres of influence?
A Afghanistan **B** Persia (Iran) **C** Turkmenistan

19. In 1908, the Austro-Hungarian Empire annexed two territories in Europe from the Ottoman Empire. They would have an important part to play in the outbreak of the First World War. What were they?

20. What was the name given to the group of political reformers who overthrew the absolutist Ottoman emperor in 1908?

21. What was first discovered in the Middle East in 1908?

22. In 1910, Mexican president Porfirio Díaz, who had been in power for thirty-one years, fixed the result of an election in his favour. What happened next?

23. When the Union of South Africa was formed in 1910 by several colonies uniting, approximately how much land was reserved for the white minority of the new country?
A Ten per cent **B** Fifty per cent **C** Ninety per cent

24. True or false? Following a republican revolution in Portugal, there were forty-five different governments between 1910 and 1926.

25. In which revolutionary war did Pancho Villa and Emiliano Zapata fight?

26. In 1911, what came to an end after 2,000 years in China?

27. Following a transitional period during which General Yuan Shikai tried to take control of the country, which organization tried to form a government in China?

28. By 1912, this Georgian/Russian revolutionary, born Joseph Dzhugashvali, was using the name Stalin. What does Stalin mean?

man of steel

29. Which of these was not a member of the Balkan League, an alliance that fought the first Balkan War in 1912 against the Ottoman Empire, freeing most of the Balkan peninsula from the Ottomans? Bulgaria, Greece, Montenegro, Serbia, Slovakia.

30. By 1914, what percentage of habitable land on Earth did European countries control?
A Twenty per cent **B** Fifty per cent **C** Eighty-five per cent.

31. In 1914, which people published a manifesto demanding independence from the Ottoman Empire?

32. True or false? The spark that ignited the First World War was the assassination of the heir to the German Empire by a Polish separatist in Warsaw.

33. True or false? Germany had prepared the Schlieffen Plan, which was a detailed scheme to quickly defeat France by a two-pronged attack across the German–French border and through Belgium.

34. True or false? In the First World War, the early German advance through Belgium pushed the Allies back to the Marne river just fifty kilometres (thirty miles) from Paris. In organizing the counter-attack that forced Germans back, French reserves were taken to the front by taxi.

35. Russia surprised Germany by mobilizing quickly and invading East Prussia. What was the name of the battle in August 1914, during which Germany repulsed the Russians?
A Tannenberg **B** Teutoburger **C** Tannenbaum

36. What was the 'Race to the Sea' in September and October 1914?

37. During the First World War, which countries were unlucky enough to contain the Western Front and this sort of warfare?

38. Poison gas (chlorine) was used by the Germans for the first time at the Second Battle of Ypres in April 1915. True or false? When the French saw the gas cloud, they thought it was a smokescreen to hide a German attack, so called for reinforcements, which simply meant that more men were exposed to the gas.

39. In 1915, Italy joined the Allied side on the expectation of receiving Austro-Hungarian territories on its border. From then until 1917, Italy fought a series of battles with Austro-Hungary along the Isonzo river in Slovenia and Italy. How many battles of Isonzo were there?
A Two **B** Five **C** Twelve

40. In 1915, the Ottomans began a systematic massacre of which people?

41. As soon as the Ottoman Empire declared for Germany and Austro-Hungary in the First World War, Britain formed the Egypt Expeditionary Force. Its objective was to safeguard which vital transport link?
A The Red Sea Steamboats **B** The Trans-Arabian Railway
C The Suez Canal

42. True or false? Britain's Egypt Expeditionary Force included a corps mounted on elephants.

43. In 1915, Britain persuaded the most important Arab leader, Hussein, the Emir of Mecca, to attack Turkish railways and supply lines. What did Britain offer in return for the Arab aid?

44. Who was the British intelligence officer sent to work with the Arabs against the Turks?

45. Where did the disastrous Allied attack on Turkey take place that led to the loss of thousands of British, French, Australian, Indian, Senegalese and New Zealand troops?

46. Who led the Turkish defence of that area?

47. What was the British secretary of state for war, Lord Kitchener, appealing for British men to do in this wartime poster?

48. Which American industrialist said in 1916, 'History is more or less bunk'? Clue: he also said, 'You can have . . . any color – so long as it's black.'

49. What was the longest battle of the First World War, running from February to December 1916? The main protagonists were the Germans and the French.
A Mons **B** Verdun **C** Cambrai

50. Which battle or 'offensive' was this that took place between 1 July and 18 November 1916?

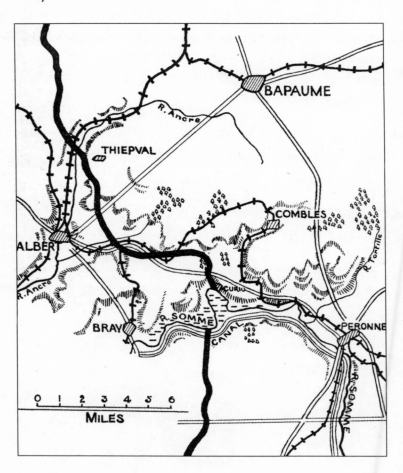

51. What was the name of the newspaper produced by British troops in the trenches during the First World War?

52. Why were German submarines named U-boats?

53. What was the 1916 Sykes-Picot Agreement?

54. What was the nickname of Germany's Manfred von Richthofen, the top-scoring fighter pilot during the First World War?

55. In what month and year did the United States join the Allies and enter the First World War?

56. Who was the American president when the USA entered the First World War?
A Theodore Roosevelt **B** Franklin D. Roosevelt
C Woodrow Wilson

57. The USA's entry into the First World War was partly inspired by its outrage when the 'Zimmermann Telegram' was uncovered by British Intelligence in January 1917. This was an approach by Germany to Mexico proposing an alliance. What did Germany suggest that Mexico could gain if it helped defeat the Allies?

58. The Battle of Passchendaele, from July to November 1917, was the most costly of the battles in Flanders, with total casualties of 850,000. Which gas was used by the Germans for the first time in this battle?

59. The Battle of Passchendaele was one of a series of battles at Ypres. Which number was it?
A The First Battle of Ypres **B** The Second Battle of Ypres
C The Third Battle of Ypres

60. Who was the last Tsar of Imperial Russia?

61. Which doomed royal family is this?

62. Why is the Russian Revolution of October 1917 known as the Bolshevik or October Revolution, also called the November Revolution?

63. Who was this first leader of Communist Russia?

64. What does USSR, the name that Communist Russia took in 1922, stand for?

65. What does the word 'soviet' mean?

66. What was the 1917 Balfour Declaration that had major repercussions in the Middle East?

67. At what time and date did the fighting officially stop in the First World War?

68. Where was the armistice between Germany and the Allies signed in 1918, at the end of the First World War?

69. The map of Europe (below) was completely redrawn after the First World War, with several new countries created. Finland, Estonia, Czechoslovakia and Yugoslavia were some of the new states formed. Which country, marked 1, was given its independence after many years of submission to powerful neighbours, but in addition was given a corridor of land, leading to the Baltic Sea, that cut part of Prussia off from Germany?

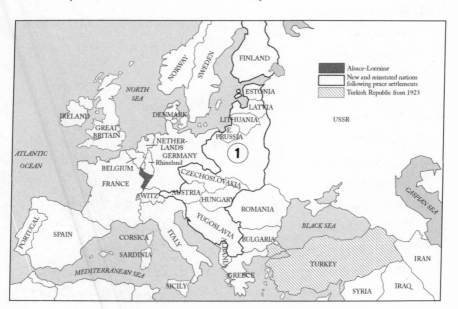

70. Why did the war on the Eastern Front end earlier than on the Western Front?

71. What was the name of the treaty that formally ended the First World War?

72. In which room was the treaty that ended the First World War signed?
A Hall of Lights **B** Hall of Flames **C** Hall of Mirrors

73. True or false? The treaty that ended the First World War broke up the territories of the German, Austrian and Ottoman empires, and required Germany to pay reparations?

74. Approximately how many people were killed in the First World War?
A 1.5 million **B** 15 million **C** 150 million.

75. When women won the right to vote in Britain in 1918, all men over the age of twenty-one could vote. What restrictions were put on women voters?

76. What was China's May the Fourth Movement in 1919?

77. What happened to Arab countries such as Palestine and Syria after the First World War?

78. When the victorious Allies divided the lands of the Ottoman Empire, they paid no attention to existing tribal, ethnic or sectarian borders. Iraq, for example, was formed from three Ottoman provinces, each dominated by a different group. What were these three groups, amongst whom conflicts continue within Iraq to the present day?

79. Who was this Arab prince, a son of the Emir of Mecca, who fought the Ottomans for Britain in the First World War, then struggled against French control of Syria, and eventually accepted the role of ruler of Iraq under the League of Nations mandate that gave Britain overall control?
A Aladdin
B Ali Baba
C Feisal

80. What happened to the German kaiser or emperor at the end of the First World War?

81. What was the name of the government that succeeded the German Empire in 1919?

82. In 1919, what killed more people than the First World War?

83. After the Anglo-Irish War from 1919 to 1921, southern Ireland won independence from Britain. What was the first name of the new state?

84. Which international organization, the forerunner of the United Nations, was founded in 1920?

85. Because of the impact of the First World War, in 1920 one of Europe's royal families changed its name from Saxe-Coburg-Saalfeld, derived from a German ancestor, to a more nationalistic name. To which country did this royal family belong?

86. A few years earlier, another European royal family had also changed their name from the Germanic sounding Saxe-Coburg and Gotha to one that reflected their nationality. What nationality was that royal family, and what name did they choose?

87. In 1920, who became leader of the Indian National Congress, an organization that campaigned for greater Indian involvement in government of the country?

88. True or false? In the early 1920s, while European countries struggled to rebuild their economies, the USA enjoyed an economic boom, partly fuelled by European nations repaying war loans.

89. What name is given to the social and economic boom time of the mid-1920s as economies recovered?

90. Who became the leader of Germany's Nazi Party in 1921?

91. What does the word 'Nazi' stand for?

92. From 1921 to 1923, which European country saw its currency so devalued that people ended up having to cart their wages home in wheelbarrows?

93. What was this discovery, made in Egypt in 1922?

94. What name is given to Hitler's attempted coup in Munich in November 1923?
A Dancehall Putsch
B Beer Hall Putsch
C Bowling Alley Putsch

95. What name did the South African Native National Congress adopt in 1923?

96. What was the name of Adolf Hitler's political memoir that laid out his basic philosophy?

97. True or false? Hitler blamed the economic woes of Germany on Jewish big businesses, Communists, and the harsh conditions of the Treaty of Versailles?

98. When did the Ottoman Empire become the Republic of Turkey?
A 1918 B 1920 C 1923

99. As was the custom in South Africa in the 1920s, when the boy Rolihlahla of the Xhosa people first went to school, he was given a new European first name, in his case the surname of a British admiral. Who is Rolihlahla better known as?

100. After a power struggle following the death of Lenin in 1924, who solidified his grip on the USSR and became effective dictator?

ANSWERS

1. **B** Quantum physics.

2. Nepal.

3. They federated as the Commonwealth of Australia.

4. True.

5. **C** *Entente Cordiale.*

6. Made the first powered flight.

7. True.

8. **B** Thomas Hardy in *The Dynasts.*

9. **C** The Japanese navy. The incident took place during the Russo-Japanese War of 1904–5, and the Russians feared that Japanese torpedo boats could be anywhere.

10. Norway and Sweden.

11. The battleship *Potemkin.*

12. He accepted an elected legislative body, the Duma, which was the first step towards an elected parliamentary government. However, he then restricted its powers.

13. **C** George Santayana.

14. Albert Einstein, and in 1905 he published four hugely significant papers, including his theory of special relativity and his description of light photons.

15. True.

16. True.

17. Russia.

18. B Persia.

19. Bosnia and Herzegovina.

20. Young Turks.

21. Oil, in Persia (Iran).

22. The Mexican Revolution.

23. C Ninety per cent.

24. True.

25. The 1910 Mexican Revolution.

26. Imperial rule was overturned in the Chinese Revolution.

27. The Nationalist Party, the Kuomintang or KMT.

28. 'Man of Steel'.

29. Slovakia.

30. C Eighty-five per cent.

31. The Arabs.

32. False. The spark was the assassination of Archduke Franz Ferdinand, Austria's heir apparent, by a Serbian nationalist in the Bosnian capital of Sarajevo.

33. True. The plan included a meticulous timetable, but real life did not follow the schedule.

34. True. They travelled to Paris by train and onwards by taxi.

35. A Tannenberg.

36. The attempt by both sides to envelope the rear of the enemy's northern wing. This resulted in both armies shifting towards the North Sea and ended with the stalemate of the trenches of the Western Front.

37. France and Belgium, where the trenches were dug.

38. True. The extra troops were sent to stations right in the line of the poison gas.

39. **C** Twelve.

40. Armenians.

41. The Suez Canal.

42. False. There was, however, a Camel Corps Brigade.

43 To support Arab independence from the Ottomans.

44. Thomas Edward Lawrence (Lawrence of Arabia).

45. The Gallipoli peninsula.

46. Mustafa Kemal, who would go on to have a glittering political career.

47. He was asking men to volunteer for the army.

48. Henry Ford. For the colour choice, he was referring to the Ford Model T car.

49. **B** Verdun.

50. The Somme.

51. *The Wipers Times.*

52. They were named after the German word for submarine, *Unterseeboot*, literally 'under sea boat'.

53. A plan by Britain and France that after the First World War they would divide between themselves the Arab lands then controlled by the Ottoman Empire.

54. The Bloody Red Baron.

55. April 1917.

56. **C** Woodrow Wilson.

57. Germany proposed that Mexico could regain its former territories in Texas, New Mexico and Arizona. Britain intercepted a coded message from the German foreign minister Arthur Zimmermann to the German ambassador to Mexico.

58. Mustard gas.

59. **C** The Third Battle of Ypres.

60. Nicholas II.

61. The Russian royal family, pictured before the Revolution. They were killed by revolutionaries in 1918.

62. The revolution began on 25 October according to the old Julian calendar. But in 1918, Russia adopted the new-style Gregorian calendar by losing two weeks, which put the event on 7 November.

63. Vladimir Lenin.

64. Union of Soviet Socialist Republics.

65. A council. Before the Russian revolution it meant any official council, and after the revolution it stood for an elected council.

66. A declaration by the British government supporting the establishment of a homeland for Jewish people in Palestine.

67. 11 a.m on 11 November 1918 – 'the eleventh hour of the eleventh day of the eleventh month'.

68. In a railway carriage in the forest of Compiègne, northern France. The armistice ended the fighting, but the full peace treaty was only agreed the following year.

69. Poland.

70. Following the Russian Revolution, Russia withdrew from the war and ended hostilities in March 1918.

71. The Treaty of Versailles.

72. C The Hall of Mirrors.

73. True.

74. B 15 million.

75. Women had to be property owners over the age of thirty.

76. A mass protest about the Treaty of Versailles that transferred German-occupied Chinese territories to Japan. It encouraged the growth of Communism in China.

77. They were taken from the Ottoman Empire and given to France or Britain to govern under a mandate of the League of Nations.

78. Shias, Sunnis and Kurds.

79. C Feisal.

80. Following a popular uprising he abdicated and went into exile in neutral Netherlands.

81. The Weimar Republic.

82. A worldwide flu epidemic.

83. The Irish Free State.

84. The League of Nations.

85. Belgium. The family chose a name meaning 'of Belgium'.

86. The British royal family, who changed their name to Windsor, after one of their principal homes.

87. Mahatma Gandhi.

88. True.

89. The Roaring Twenties.

90. Adolf Hitler.

91. Nationalsozialistische Deutsche Arbeiterpartei or the National Socialist German Workers' Party.

92. Germany.

93. The tomb of the pharaoh Tutankhamun.

94. B Beer Hall Putsch.

95. The African National Congress, or ANC.

96. *Mein Kampf* (My Struggle).

97. True.

98. C 1923.

99. Nelson Mandela.

100. Stalin.

CHAPTER 10

1925–1945

1. After the death of the Nationalist revolutionary Sun Yat-sen in 1925, who led the Chinese Kuomintang? *Chang Kai Shek*

2. In 1926, the Arab province of Hejaz changed its name. What is it now known as?

   A United Arab Emirates **B** Yemen **C** Saudi Arabia.

3. Who became head of the fascist government that took power in Portugal following a military coup in 1926?

   A António de Oliveira Salazar **B** Pimenta de Castro **C** Sidónio Pais

4. What conflict began in China in 1927? *Civil War*

5. What crashed in 1929, and what did it lead to? *Stock Market → Depression*

6. True or false? Following the boom years of the 1920s, by 1930 one in five Americans owned a car.

   Capone's gang killed Bugs moran gang members

7. Who killed whom in the St. Valentine's Day Massacre in Chicago in 1929?

8. In 1930, Prince Ras Tafari became emperor of Ethiopia and changed his name. What was his new name? *Haile Salassie*

9. In 1930, an Indian led a peaceful protest march in India centred around a commodity that Indians were forbidden from collecting or selling independently. What was it? *Salt*

10. True or false? In 1931, Chinese communists set up the first communist state in China, the Jiangxi Soviet.

11. Where did Japan invade in 1931, setting up a puppet government and using the territory as a springboard for a further invasion in 1937? *Manchuria*

12. This Sino-Japanese War became part of a wider conflict. What was it? *WW II*

13. True or false? In 1933, Joseph Goebbels was appointed the Nazi minister for Public Education and Propaganda.

14. In 1933, the Nazis built the first of their concentration camps, at first to hold political prisoners. Was it
    A Dachau B Auschwitz C Buchenwald?

15. What was repealed in the USA in 1933? *Prohibition Volstead Act*

16. In the power struggle for control of the German army and military forces in 1934, Hitler authorized the murder of leaders of the paramilitary stormtroopers or Sturmabteilung (the brown-shirted SA) by the SS, the Schutzstaffel (the black-shirted Protection Squadron), another military force that was loyal to Hitler and grew into the Nazis' elite troops. What was this purge known as?
    A Kristallnacht. B The Night of the Long Knives.
    C The Great Backstab

17. What name is given to this retreat in 1934–35 by the Chinese Communists during the Chinese Civil War? *long march*

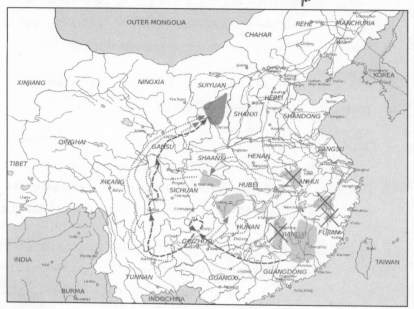

18. Which Communist leader came to prominence during this retreat, and would go on to declare the Communist People's Republic of China in 1949? *Mao Tse-Tung*

19. In 1934, Turkish people were required to take surnames for the first time. What was the surname given to Mustapha Kemal, the first president of the modern republic of Turkey, and what does it mean? *Attaturk* *father of the Turks*

20. What name was given to the series of economic reforms and federal relief programmes introduced by US president Franklin D. Roosevelt during the 1930s to alleviate the Great Depression? *New Deal*

21. In 1935, what country changed its name to the historical word meaning 'Land of the Aryans' in its own language? *Persia → Iran*

22. In what year did the Spanish Civil War begin? *1936*

23. What name was given to units of foreign men and women who supported the republicans against the fascist nationalists during the Spanish Civil War? *International Brigades*

24. Who came to power at the end of the Spanish Civil War and remained a dictator until his death in 1975? *Franco*

25. Fascist Germany supported the Spanish fascists, and the German air force, the Luftwaffe, gained experience in bombing and strafing during the Spanish Civil War. The artist Pablo Picasso painted a picture of the aftermath of Luftwaffe bombing of which Basque town? *Guernica*

26. In the 1930s, drought and inappropriate farming methods caused severe soil erosion in the American Great Plains. When caught up by winds, the soil choked the air, forcing thousands of farming families to abandon the area. What was the name given to this phenomenon? *Dust Bowl*

27. Where was the Arab Rebellion of 1936–9? *Palestine*

28. What name is given to the atrocities committed by Japanese troops in the Republic of China's capital from December 1937 to January 1938? *Rape of Nanjing*

29. In 1937, what did the Chinese Communists and Nationalists agree? *To join against Jap. invasion*

30. What was the Anschluss of 1938? *Germany's annexation of Austria*

31. The picture shows the result of a Nazi attack on Jewish synagogues and businesses on the night of 9–10 November 1938. What was this pogrom called, and why?

32. True or false? Adolf Hitler's real surname was Schicklgruber?

33. In order to prevent war, the two Allies Britain and France signed the Munich Agreement with Germany in 1938, allowing Hitler to annex which territory on his promise that this would be his last expansionist demand?

34. What name was given to this policy of the Allies to allow Hitler a certain amount of expansion?
A Acceptance **B** Allowance **C** Appeasement

35. What did the British prime minister, Neville Chamberlain, announce that the Munich Agreement would give, and was he correct?

36. True or false? Germany and its allies of Italy and Japan in the Second World War were known as the Axis powers because on a map a straight north-west to north-east line or axis could be drawn between their countries.

37. With which Eastern European country did Britain and France have alliances, so that when Germany invaded it, the Allies had to declare war?

38. On what date did Britain and France declare war on Germany? *Sept 3 1939*

39. Having re-armed and built up an air force (Luftwaffe) in defiance of the Treaty of Versailles after the First World War, Germany was able to advance quickly with tanks and armoured vehicles, covered from the air, with the infantry following on. What was this tactic called?

40. In November 1939, what did the Germans create in Warsaw, and seal off from the rest of the city? *Ghetto*

41. What was the name of the British force that was sent to support the French in 1939? *British Expeditionary Force*

42. The French forces thought they were secure behind the Maginot Line, a defensive fortification that had been built along the French–German border. How did the Nazis overcome this barrier? *went around thro Belgium*

43. In their drive through France, what did the Germans succeed in doing on 20 May 1940?

44. What name was given to these small boats – fishing boats, yachts, etc. – that answered the British Admiralty's appeal to help evacuate soldiers from France at Dunkirk?

45. Some 338,000 Allied soldiers were rescued from France in the face of the German invasion, but what did they leave behind?

46. The German invasion of Denmark and Norway in April 1940 saw what type of troops deployed for the first time in large numbers?

47. After Britain and France were forced out of Norway by the invading Germans, the British prime minister Neville Chamberlain resigned in May 1940. Who was elected prime minister in his place?

48. France surrendered to Germany in June 1940. Where was the French puppet government under the Nazis based?

49. What name was given to the German bombing of British cities from September 1940 to May 1941?

50. In what year did the Battle of Britain take place?

51. To whom was British prime minister Winston Churchill referring to his 1940 speech, 'Never in the field of human conflict was so much owed by so many to so few'?

52. Who was this French officer (right), who organized the Free French forces from Britain in 1940?

53. What did Britain introduce on 8 January 1940, which continued in some ways until 1954?

54. What weapon was used to assassinate the Russian revolutionary Leon Trotsky, who was in exile in Mexico City in August 1940?

55. During the Second World War, the French existentialist philosophers Jean-Paul Sartre and Simone de Beauvoir joined which organization?
A The French Resistance **B** The Vichy France government
C The Nazi Party

56. Which neutral European country offered a safe haven to refugees during the Second World War? Its diplomats also issued false passports to Jews in many countries.

A Sweden **B** Switzerland **C** Portugal

57. During the Second World War, there were nine formally recognized governments-in-exile in London. Which countries, occupied by the Nazis, did they represent?

France, Netherlands, Belgium, Luxembourg, Norway, Poland, Czechoslovakia, ? Denmark, Greece, Yugoslavia

58. True or false? During the Second World War there were several other exiled heads of state based in London, including Emperor Haile Selassie of Ethiopia and King Zog of Albania.

59. After the Japanese invasion of the Philippines in 1941, a Philippine government-in-exile was set up in which country?

A Australia **B** China **C** The USA

60. In the 1940s, who wrote the poem that begins 'First they came for the Communists, And I did not speak out, Because I was not a Communist' and ends with 'Then they came for me, And there was no one left, To speak out for me'?

61. Which Mediterranean island was besieged by the Germans and Italians from 1940 to 1942 because it was a strategic base for Allied planes to prevent Axis resupply of their North African Forces? After the siege was lifted, the island and its people received a collective George Cross. *Malta*

62. In June 1941, Germany turned on a former ally and invaded with four million men; the largest invasion force in history. What country was the target? *Russia*

63. What was the German operational name for this invasion? *Barbarossa*

64. Which Russian city was besieged by the Germans from September 1941 to January 1944? It was the longest siege in history. *Leningrad*

65. Where in Asia were huge Allied defensive guns, and why did they not provide the defence that was expected of them? *Singapore Faced wrong way*

66. Josip Broz was the leading Yugoslavian communist partisan leader fighting the Nazis. By what name was he usually known? *Marshall Tito*

67. The USA remained neutral in the Second World War until the Japanese launched this surprise attack on which American naval base on 7 December 1941? *Pearl Harbour*

68. Which German commander took charge of the Afrika Korps in February 1941, and what was his nickname?

Rommel Desert Fox

69. In January 1942, what chilling decision did the Nazis reach at the Wannsee Conference?

FINAL SOLUTION = Holocaust

70. What does this line indicate in 1942?

Furthorest extant of Japanese expansion

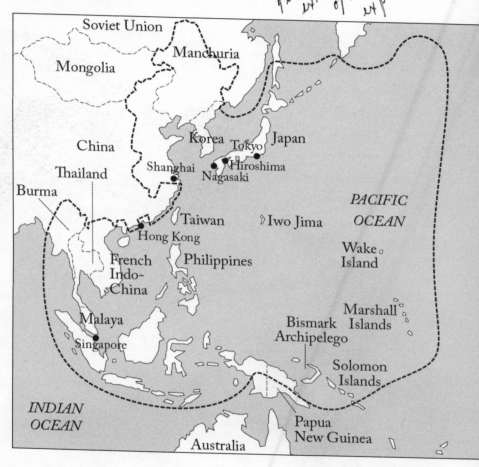

71. There were several turning points in the Second World War. What was the most important turning point in Russia?

Stalingrad

72. True or false? In July 1943, Germany and Russia fought the largest tank battle in history at Kursk. It was a Russian victory, and from then on the Red Army never lost a battle as they pressed into Germany. *T*

73. What nickname was given to William Joyce, who broadcast Nazi radio propaganda in English? *Lord HawHaw*

74. Another turning point of the war happened in North Africa in October 1942, after this new Allied commander arrived in the theatre of war and won a decisive victory. Who was he? *Monty*

75. Winston Churchill said of this crucial battle, 'Before—we never had a victory. After—we never had a defeat.' What battle was he referring to? *2nd El Alamein*

76. Victory in North Africa allowed the Allies to launch an invasion of which country
A France **B** Spain **C** Italy

77. How did the weather help the Allies crack the German Enigma naval codes? *German to weather report — always broadcast in code everyday*

78. Which future US president was in command of a Patrol Torpedo boat in the Pacific when it was rammed and sunk by a Japanese destroyer? *Kennedy*

79. Which desperate tactic was used by these Japanese pilots?

80. What was the nickname of the German V-1 flying bombs that were launched at Britain from June 1944?

81. Who was the American general who was the overall commander of the Normandy landings and the invasion of Germany? He was elected president of the USA in 1953.

82. What does the D in D-Day stand for?
A Dawn **B** Day **C** Decision.

83. What were the codenames of the five Normandy beaches targeted for the D-Day landings?

84. True or false? The news that British airborne troops had successfully landed in France on D-Day was brought back to Britain by a carrier pigeon called 'Duke of Normandy'.

85. Which three European countries came together in 1944 to form a future customs union, the Benelux Convention?

86. Which German city is shown here following carpet-bombing by the Allies in February 1945?

87. Which three heads of state met at the Yalta Conference in February 1945?

88. Which wartime leader died on 12 April 1945, and who succeeded him?

89. What final act did Hitler take on 30 April 1945?

90. True or false? On 1 May 1945, the Nazi propaganda minister Joseph Goebbels and his wife Magda killed their six children by poison before committing suicide themselves.

91. What was the unexpected result of the British general election in July 1945?

92. On 16 July 1945, the American physicist Robert Oppenheimer quoted from the Hindu scripture, the *Bhagavad Gita*: 'Now I am become death, the destroyer of worlds.' What was he reacting to?

93. On which Japanese city was the first atomic bomb dropped on 6 August 1945?

94. What city was the target of the second atomic bomb on 9 August 1945?

95. Where was the official Japanese surrender on 2 September 1945 signed?

96. The Nazis put the slogan '*Arbeit macht frei*' above the gates to Auschwitz and several other concentration camps. What does this mean?

97. What percentage of the world's population was involved in the Second World War?
A Twenty-five per cent **B** Fifty per cent **C** Seventy-five per cent

98. At the end of the Second World War, what did the Communists and Nationalists do in China?

99. In November 1945, the trials for war crimes of several Nazi leaders began. In what city did they take place?

100. After the Second World War, with much of Europe and Asia either devastated or economically exhausted, what was the richest nation in the world?
A Canada **B** The USA **C** Argentina

ANSWERS

1. Chiang Kai-shek.

2. **C** Saudi Arabia.

3. **A** António de Oliveira Salazar.

4. The Civil War between the Communists and the Nationalists (Kuomintang) who had control over most of China.

5. New York's Wall Street stock exchange, leading to the Great Depression.

6. True.

7. Members of Al Capone's criminal gang shot seven members of a rival gang led by George 'Bugs' Moran.

8. Haile Selassie.

9. Salt.

10. True. The Communists were forced out in 1934 by the Nationalists in the Chinese Civil War.

11. Manchuria in north-east China.

12. The Second World War.

13. True. The Nazis were experts at persuading people to follow the party line.

14. **A** Dachau.

15. Prohibition.

16. **B** The Night of the Long Knives.

17. The Long March.

18. Mao Zedong.

19. Ataturk, 'Father of the Turks'.

20. The New Deal.

21. Persia changed its name to Iran.

22. 1936.

23. The International Brigades.

24. General Francisco Franco.

25. Guernica.

26. The Dust Bowl.

27. Palestine, which was at the time controlled by Britain under a Mandate from the League of Nations. The Arabs were protesting about increasing Jewish immigration and land purchases.

28. The Rape of Nanjing.

29. To suspend hostilities and unite against the Japanese invaders.

30. Germany's annexation of Austria, part of the Nazis' plan to unify all German-speaking parts of Europe.

31. Kristallnacht (Crystal Night) or 'Night of the Broken Glass' because of the amount of shattered windowpanes left lying on the streets after the attacks.

32. False. This was Allied propaganda meant to make Hitler sound foolish, although one of his grandmothers was indeed called Maria Schicklgruber.

33. The Sudetenland, the German-speaking part of Czechoslovakia. Czechoslovakia was not consulted about this decision.

34. Appeasement.

35. 'Peace in our time', and he was completely wrong since Hitler went on to demand the Baltic free port of Danzig (now Gdansk) in Poland.

36. False. The name derived from the alliance formed in 1936 between Germany and Italy that was known as the Rome–Berlin Axis.

37. Poland.

38. 3 September 1939.

39. Blitzkrieg or 'lightning war'.

40. The Warsaw Ghetto for Jews.

41. The British Expeditionary Force (BEF).

42. They went through Belgium, especially the Ardennes forest, bursting through the lightly fortified lines of defence.

43. They split the Allied forces in two and forced the British back to the French coast.

44. The Little Ships.

45. Almost all their weapons and military equipment.

46. Paratroopers.

47. Winston Churchill.

48. Vichy.

49. The Blitz.

50. 1940.

51. The Royal Air Force and other airmen who fought the German planes in the Battle of Britain.

52. Charles de Gaulle.

53. Rationing.

54. An ice-pick.

55. A The French Resistance.

56. Portugal.

57. Belgium, Czechoslovakia, France, Greece, Luxembourg, the Netherlands, Norway, Poland and Yugoslavia.

58. True.

59. A Australia.

60. The German pastor, Martin Niemöller.

61. Malta.

62. The USSR.

63. Operation Barbarossa.

64. Leningrad.

65. The British colony of Singapore, and they were pointed out to sea, loaded with ammunition for firing on ships. The Japanese invaded in 1941 by land through the Malaysian peninsula, which the British had thought would be impenetrable.

66. Tito.

67. Pearl Harbor in Hawaii.

68. Erwin Rommel, the 'Desert Fox'.

69. A policy that they called the 'Final Solution', the systematic murder of Jews in death camps or by other means.

70. The greatest extent of Japanese expansion.

71. The Battle of Stalingrad from August 1942 to February 1943. Although at first the Germans pressed the Russians back to the Volga river, the Red Army launched a surprise, two-pronged attack and encircled the Nazi forces in the city, forcing them to surrender.

72. True.

73. Lord Haw-Haw.

74. General Bernard Montgomery.

75. The Second Battle of El Alamein.

76. C Italy.

77. The German word for weather, *wetter*, was broadcast in code every day at the same time to announce daily weather forecasts, giving the codebreakers a base to start from.

78. John F. Kennedy.

79. The kamikaze suicide attacks by Japanese planes on Allied naval vessels.

80. Doodlebugs.

81. Dwight D. Eisenhower.

82. B Day.

83. Gold, Juno, Omaha, Sword and Utah.

84. True.

85. Belgium, the Netherlands and Luxembourg.

86. Dresden.

87. Stalin of the USSR, Franklin D. Roosevelt of the USA and Winston Churchill of the UK.

88. US President Franklin D. Roosevelt, succeeded by his vice president, Harry S. Truman.

89. He shot himself in his bunker in Berlin.

90. True.

91. Clement Atlee's Labour Party defeated wartime prime minister Winston Churchill and his Conservative Party.

92. The first atomic bomb detonation in the Trinity Test, New Mexico.

93. Hiroshima.

94. Nagasaki.

95. On board the American battleship USS *Missouri* in Tokyo Bay.

96. 'Work sets you free.'

97. **C** Seventy-five per cent.

98. Resume the Civil War, leading to Communist victory in 1949.

99. Nuremberg.

100. **B** The USA.

PICTURE CREDITS

by C. Strahlheim, Frankfurt, 1834 -1840.

Page 59: Fresco of *The Coronation of Charlemagne* by Raphael, Room of the Fire in the Borgo, Vatican Museum; photo Viacheslav Lopatin / Shutterstock.com.

Page 60: A political map of Europe featuring areas of major Viking incursions and the dates of famous Viking raids / Adhavoc (CC BY-SA 3.0).

Page 63: Map of the Khazar Empire 600 -850 A.D., public domain.

Page 70: Map showing the extent of the Chola Empire during the reign of Rajendra Chola I; illustration by Venu62 / en.wikipedia (CC BY-SA 3.0).

Page 71: Scene from the Bayeux Tapestry showing King Harold receiving an arrow in his eye; illustration from *The Story of the World* by Elizabeth O'Neill, New York, 1910.

Page 72: Map of the Seljuk Dynasty (1037-1194 A.D. via the Arab League at English Wikipedia / public domain.

Page 73: Photo of a Chichen Itza chacmool by CampPhoto / iStock

Page 74: Lone moai standing on Easter Island; photo Tero Hakala / Shutterstock.com

Page 75: Map to illustrate the principal routes of the first four Crusades from *Outlines of the World's History* by William Swinton, American Book Company, 1902.

Page 76: Illustration of Frederick Barbarossa from Clipart.com (*top*); portrait of Saladin on a Syrian banknote (1991); photo vkilikov / Shutterstock.com (*bottom*).

Page 78: Illustration, by John Leech, of King John refusing to sign the Magna Carta when first presented to him, published 1875: image Everett Historical / Shutterstock.com.

Page 81: Map showing the Mongol Empire at its greatest extent ca. 1300 from *Historical Atlas* by William Shepherd, New York, 1911.

Page 82: *Macbeth, Shakespeare: the three weird sisters* by Henry Fuseli / Wellcome Images (CC BY-SA 3.0).

Page 83: Illustration from *Dolls of the Tusayan Indians* by Jesse Walter Fewkes, publisher E. J. Brill, Boston and Leiden, 1894.

Page 84: Spread of the Black Death in medieval Europe; map Andy85719 (CC BY-SA 3.0) (*top*); jar with dragon, Ming dynasty, early 15th century; gift of Robert E. Tod, 1937 / Metropolitan Museum of Art, New York (*bottom*).

Page 93: Plan of the Battle of Agincourt from *The Art of War in the Middle Ages* by Charles Oman, Oxford, 1885.

Page 94: Illustration of Hiawatha by Frederic Remington from *The Song of Hiawatha* by Henry Wadsworth Longfellow, Houghton, Mifflin & Co., Cambridge, Mass., 1890.

Page 95: A bust of Vlad Tepes, Vlad the Impaler, the inspiration for Dracula, in the Old Princely Court, Curtea Veche, Bucharest, Romania: photo douglasmack / Shutterstock.com.

Page 96: France in the late 15th Century', from *Muir's Historical Atlas: Medieval and Modern*, London, 1911; map adapted by Zigeuner (CC BY-SA 3.0).

Page 97: Map showing Africa and the Songhai Empire; Universal Images Group North America LLC / Alamy.

Page 98: Treaty of Tordesillas, 1494; map showing the Treaty line / Ultimadesigns at English Wikibooks.

Page 102: Map of the Mughal Empire from *India: a country study* / Federal Research Division, Library of Congress (*top*); map of Brazil in 1534 showing the administrative divisions / Shadowxfox (CC BY-SA 4.0) (*bottom*).

Page 103: Head of an Oba, Nigeria, Court of Benin; The Michael C. Rockefeller Memorial Collection, Bequest of Nelson A. Rockefeller, 1979 / Metropolitan Museum of Art, New York.

Page 105: Fresco depicting the Battle of Lepanto in 1571 and showing Don Juan of Austria and the cardinals, Franciscan Church of the Visitation, Ein Karem, Israel; photo Abraham (CC BY-SA 3.0).

Page 114: Defenestration of Prague, 1618, wood engraving published in 1881; image ZU_09 / iStock.

Page 115: Engraving showing the Pilgrim Fathers leaving Delfshaven in the Netherlands in 1620 / Clipart.com.

Page 116: Portrait of Cardinal Richelieu by Philippe de Champaigne, the Louvre Museum, Paris; photo Everett Historical / Shutterstock.com.

Page 117: Map of Bohemia from CIA Publications / *The World Factbook*.

Page 119: Portrait of Louis XIV by the Hyacinthe Rigaud studio, 1701; photo Everett – Art / Shutterstock.com.

Page 123: Map from *The Colonies 1492-1750* by Reuben Gold Thwaites, New York, 1910 (*top*); the Mission San Luis Obispo de Tolosa, a Californian landmark since 1772; photo Marty Nelson / Shutterstock.com (bottom).

Page 124: Engraving of George Washington published in *The Gallery of Portraits With Memoirs*, 1837; image Georgios Kollidas / Shutterstock.com.

Page 125: King George III, ca. 1760s; image Everett Historical / Shutterstock.com.

Page 126: The Storming of the Bastille, 1789; illustration Everett Historical / Shutterstock.com.

Page 128: Map of the 'Triangular Trade' between Britain, its American colonies and Africa in the 17th and 18th centuries; illustration Granger Historical Picture Archive / Alamy.

Page 134: Map from *An Elementary History of our Country* by Eva March Tappan, Houghton, Mifflin & Co., 1922.

Page 135: Route of the Lewis and Clark Expedition; map Victor van Werkhooven / public domain.

Page 136: A statue of the Duke of Wellington located in the historic city of Norwich, UK; photo chrisdorney / Shutterstock.com.

Page 137: Map of Napoleon's Russian campaign from *The Life of Napoleon I* by John Holland Rose, G. Bell and Sons Ltd., London, 1910.

Page 138: Map of the Battle of Waterloo *A Brief History of Europe from 1789 to 1815* by Lucius Holt, Alexander Chilton and William Harrison, The Macmillan Company, New York, 1919.

Page 140: Statue of Simon Bolivar, founder of La Gran Colombia, in Iber-American Plaza, Central Station, Sydney, Australia; photo Sourabh / Shutterstock.com

Page 141: Map of Gran Colombia, 1819; Shadowxfox (CC BY-SA 3.0)

Page 143: A 1975 British postage stamp celebrating the 150th Anniversary of the Public Railways with the founding of the Stockton and Darlington Railway, 1825; image Andy Lidstone / Shutterstock.com.

Page 146: The Alamo in San Antonio, Texas; photo Steven Frame / Shutterstock.com

Page 148: Map showing the industrialisation of Western Europe from *A History of Europe from the Reformation to the Present Day* by Ferdinand Schevill, New York, 1923.

Page 156: Illustration of the Charge of the Light Brigade, Battle of Balaclava, 1854, from the Illustrated London News.

Page 158: Map of Italy in 1861 from Clipart.com.

Page 159: Portrait of Abraham Lincoln; photo Everett Historical / Shutterstock.com.

Page 160: Contemporary map of the Battle of Gettysburg, July 3 1863; image Andrew_Howe / iStock.

Page 161: Buffalo soldiers of the 25th Infantry or the 9th Cavalry, while stationed at Yosemite National Park, ca. 1899; photo Everett Historical / Shutterstock.com.

Page 162: *The Driving of the Last Spike*, 1881, a painting by Thomas Hill depicting the ceremony held at Promontory Point, Utah, on May 10, 1869, marking the completion of the transcontinental railroad; photo Everett Historical / Shutterstock.com.

Page 164: Photo of Zulu warriors from the Bain Collection / Library of Congress Prints and Photographs Division (LC-DIG-ggbain-00042).

Page 166: Contemporary photo of the eruption of Krakatoa, taken from a passing ship, public domain (top); portrait of Geronimo, Chiricahua Apache warrior in 1898, when he was held with his family at Fort Sill, Oklahoma; photo Everett Historical / Shutterstock.com (bottom).

Page 167: Statue of Liberty, New York; photo UbjsP / Shutterstock.com.

Page 168: Map of Vietnam by Peter Hermes Furian / iStock.

Page 169: Map of Ethiopia by Peter Hermes Furian / Shutterstock.com.

Page 171: USA Central Intelligence Agency map of Thailand (2002) / Library of Congress Geography and Map Division (item 2005632335).

Page 181: Portrait of Albert Einstein / Library of Congress Prints and Photographs Division (LC-USZ62-106042).

Page 182: Photo of Joseph Stalin from Clipart.com.

Page 184: British WWI machine gun crew in a front line trench, 1914-18: photo Everett Historical / Shutterstock.com.

Page 185: WWI poster by Alfred Leete / Library of Congress Prints and Photographs Division (LC-DIG-ppm-sca-37468).

Page 186: Map of the Somme battlefield from *The Somme, Volume I: The First Battle of the Somme (1916 -1917)*, Michelin & Cie., 1919.

Page 188: Russian Royal family in 1914 (left to right seated: Marie, Queen Alexandra, Czar Nicholas II, Anastasia, Alexei; standing: Olga and Tatiana; photo Everett Historical / Shutterstock.com (*top*); statue of Lenin, Moscow Square, St. Petersburg; photo Vinokurov Kirill / Shuttestock.com (*bottom*).

Page 189: Europe and the Middle East after the peace settlements of 1918 and the formation of the Turkish Republic in 1923; map by David Woodroffe from *The 20th Century in Bite-sized Chunks*, Michael O'Mara Books Ltd., 2016.

Page 191: Portrait of Faisal I, king of Iraq in 1921-1933; photo by APIC / Getty Images.

Page 193: Howard Carter, English egyptologist, pictured near the golden sarcophagus of Tutankhamun in Egypt, 1922; photo Harry Burton / APIC / Getty Images.

Page 202: The route of the Long March in China, 1934-1935; map Rowanwindwhistler / Ericmetro (CC BY-SA 3.0).

Page 204: Windows of a Jewish-owned business smashed during Kristallnacht, Berlin, November 9-10, 1938; photo Everett Historical / Shutterstock.com.

Page 205: The Maginot Line in France / Goran tek-en (CC BY-SA 3.0)

Page 206: Photo of World War II Dunkirk evacuation from Clipart.com.

Page 207: General de Gaulle saluting the guard of honour on his visit to Tunisia, 1943 / Library of Congress Prints and Photographs Division (LC-DIG-fsa-8d32420).

Page 209: Pearl Harbour, Hawaii; USS West Virginia aflame / Library of Congress Prints and Photographs Division (LC-USW33-018432-C)

Page 210: The extent of Japanese expansion by 1942; map by David Woodroffe from *The 20th Century in Bite-sized Chunks*, Michael O'Mara Books Ltd., 2016.

Page 211: Field Marshal Bernard L. Montgomery watches his tanks move up, North Africa, November 1942 / US National Archives (ID: 208-PU-138LL-3, War and Conflict Book No. 1017).

Page 212: Japanese kamikaze pilots. Kamikaze, 'Divine Wind', refers to a typhoon that swept Mongol invaders away from the Japanese coast in 1286; photo © Hulton-Deutsch Collection / Corbis via Getty Images.

Page 213: Bodies in the street after the allied fire bombing of Dresden, Germany, February 1945; photo Keystone / Hulton Archive / Getty Images.